On Earth as in Heaven

Also by Dorothee Soelle
Published by Westminster/John Knox Press

The Strength of the Weak:
Toward a Christian Feminist Identity

On Earth as in Heaven

A Liberation Spirituality of Sharing

Dorothee Soelle

Translated by Marc Batko

Westminster/John Knox Press
Louisville, Kentucky

Unless otherwise noted, scripture quotations are from the New Revised Standard Version of the Bible, copyright © 1989 by the Division of Christian Education of the National Council of the Churches of Christ in the U.S.A., and are used by permission.

Book design by Drew Stevens

Cover illustration: Taller "Jesus Obrero," El Salvador

Cover design by Laura Lee

First edition

This book is printed on acid-free paper that meets the American National Standards Institute Z39.48 standard. ∞

Published by Westminster/John Knox Press
Louisville, Kentucky

PRINTED IN THE UNITED STATES OF AMERICA
9 8 7 6 5 4 3 2 1

Library of Congress Cataloging-in-Publication Data

Sölle, Dorothee.
    On Earth as in heaven : a liberation spirituality of sharing /
    Dorothee Soelle ; translated by Marc Batko. — 1st ed.
        p.   cm.
    ISBN 0–664–25494–2 (pbk. : alk. paper)

    1. Freedom (Theology)   2. Christianity and justice.
3. Spirituality.   I. Title.
BT810.2.S64   1993
261.8—dc20   93–1314

Contents

Translator's Note

Dorothee Soelle offers a new way of doing theology, the way of narrative and dialogue, which has more power than the way of dogmatics and propositional systematic theology. Instead of receiving truths "from above," the reader is actively part of the search for truth and is summoned to both the biblical and the contemporary global context.

The truth of liberating spirituality possesses us more than we possess it and is more an unfinished process than a weapon of domination. Interwoven with personal experiences, prayers, and knowledge gained from other cultures and faiths, Professor Soelle's approach is multicultural and self-critical, enlivened by insights from Native Americans and black spirituals. In this theology of liberation, the poor are continually our teachers, and solidarity is the fruit of love.

The feminine qualities of God are underlined in Dorothee Soelle's theology. No longer is God confined to the masculine categories of lord, master, and warrior; God is warmth, tenderness, and nearness. The bloody history of hierarchical Christianity is overcome by the history of resistance and the vision of a church from below. As the early church related differently to property and the state (as well as state violence), we are also called to see with new global eyes and to plead for justice, reconciliation, and peace in a divided world.

Estrangement from nature and history can be healed. Our broken bodies and spirits can be re-membered. New perspectives, hopes, and consciousness can supplant the myths and distortions of a theology of glory that avoids evil, suffering, poverty, and death. Only when the church sees its unholiness, can it see the sacredness of all creation. "Theology has to make us hungry for the reign of God. Then a fragment of change can appear," proclaims Dorothee Soelle.

"A book must be like an axe to break the frozen soul"
(Kafka). In emphasizing the narrative and liberating powers
of theology, Dorothee Soelle's perspectives enable us to speak
of faith, vision, and remembrance with new credibility. God
and the work of human liberation are seen as present and
future harbingers of a healed world combating the distortions of racism, sexism, and domination. "Love is a light that
will never go out, a light of acceptance and new creation."
"Out of the suffering history of shame and guilt will come
the vision of a liberated Europe in which plowshares are
forged out of swords."

Dorothee Soelle challenges us to a new language of truth.
As Dietrich Bonhoeffer prophesied nearly fifty years ago from
a Tegel prison, "The time will come when people will speak
the word of God and the world will be changed, a new language of truth and justice as Jesus spoke, in a way that scan-
dalizes and draws people, not religious but liberating. . . . "

A translator is like one discovering another country. Un-
covering what is concealed, a translator must do justice to
both the writer and the reader. I thank my friends Clif Ross,
Bob Forsberg, John Lind, and Ben Clarke, as well as West-
minster/John Knox Press, for their corrections, enthusiasm,
and encouragement.

MARC BATKO

Acknowledgments

"Street People in the U.S.A." From *Junge Kirche* 51 (May 1990), 295–96.

"The Future of the Poor." From *Gottes Zukunft—Zukunft der Welt*, Festschrift for Jürgen Moltmann, edited by Hermann Deuser, Gerhard Marcel Martin, Konrad Stock, and Michael Welker, 404–13. Munich: Chr. Kaiser Verlag, 1986.

"Jesus and Women's Self-Acceptance." From *Neue Wege* 82 (March 1988), 76–81.

"People Without Vision Perish." Translation of "Ein Volk ohne Vision geht zugrunde" (unpublished, 1989).

"On Earth as in the West." From *Junge Kirche* 52 (July 1991), 405.

"Moses, Jesus, and Marx: Utopians in Search of Justice." From *Junge Kirche* 52 (May 1991), 261–67.

"God's Second Creation." From *Junge Kirche* 50 (Dec. 1989), 735–38.

"The Christmas Gospel: Luke 2:1–20." From *Junge Kirche* 51 (Nov. 1990), 640–41.

"In Search of a New Religious Language." From *Wort und Antwort* 31 (July–Sept. 1990), 100–105.

"Freedom as Thirst for Liberation." From *Junge Kirche* 50 (April 1989), 210–14.

"Prayer Based on the Ninetieth Psalm." From *Junge Kirche* 50 (July–August 1989), 418–19.

Introduction

"On Earth as in Heaven" is a prayer, not a statement. It claims our hope for this world and for ourselves: there will be a time when God's will or dream will be done not only in God's realm among cherubim and seraphim but on earth among principalities and powers as well. To pray does not mean to ask someone else to fulfill, instead of us, what we cannot bring forward. It means to cooperate with God, it asks that we may be empowered and commissioned. We may say God has a dream about us humans; in prayer we end letting God dream alone, we participate in God's dream, we join.

Sometimes I fear this becomes harder and harder. In reflecting on the title of this book I recalled a meeting with students from the former East Germany. I asked them how they had lived through the turning, the unforeseen change, this nonviolent revolution. I was eager to hear something about the role of the church in the events. A timid young woman responded out of her perspective from a town near the Baltic Sea. Even there people gathered for "Monday prayers," meetings in the church for reflection, debate, Bible readings, strategizing, and prayer. The church was full as never before or later. "How did you feel about it?" I asked, knowing that she was a Lutheran Christian. "We ended up by praying the Our Father. There were young people on my right and on my left side. They did not know the words of the Lord's Prayer. I guess they had come to church for the first time in their lives. It was hard for me to pray aloud without the murmuring on my side. I did not want to be separated from my neighbors. However, I was."

Will this separation of those who yearn for a different freedom grow? Are we capable of communicating our hopes? I find it sometimes hard enough to communicate my fears, to share my nightmares. How dare I say a word of hope? I need to ground heaven on earth. (*Den Himmel erden!*) The best ally in this crazy enterprise that we sometimes call "faith" I find in the Bible. The book tells me the story of God's covenant with us under realistic conditions.

I would like to introduce the reader of this book to the hermeneutical approach I use. How are we to do theology in a meaningful—that is, life-changing—way? My proposal is grounded in different liberation theologies and moves in a four-step program. I call them praxis, analysis, meditation, and renewed praxis. My hope is that the reader will make out all four ingredients in going through this book. To put it more humbly, I hope for a reader who will at least miss those parts he or she does not find.

Whereas traditional theology starts with the text (the Word of God, the gospel), liberation theology starts with the context of our lives, our experiences, our hopes and fears, our "praxis." This is not to deny the power of the text and its spiritual quality, but to make room for it.

In order to understand our own praxis, we have to listen and to see and to feel. None of it is given. The descriptive has to touch the depth of our feelings. The first question to ask about our praxis is: "Who is victimized?" The literary form will be the narrative or the descriptive. Our concern, our worrying becomes visible in the process. We have to expose ourselves personally and increase our vulnerability. The goal of the first step is to make us see the Cross.

When we listen to the cry that comes out of praxis we develop a need for the best available analysis. The second step is to understand, to identify the causes, to name the Beast. The analytical question then becomes: "Who profits?" The literary form is the socioeconomic analysis. We move from the personal experience to the institutional analysis. We make use of other materials and broaden our experiential understanding, but by asking all the whys we ground our understanding in the depth of the historical process. The goal of the second step is to recognize the Principalities and Powers.

The narrative and the analytical together constitute the context. We should withstand the temptation to leap too early into the text, which then would be a "leaning on the everlasting arms" without foundation in the historical and institutional realities. In order to dialogue with the Word of God, the praxis of the prophets and Jesus, we need the clearest understanding of our own praxis. When we delve deep enough into our own situation, we will reach a point where theological reflection becomes necessary. We then have to "theologize" the given situation. We read the context (steps 1 and 2) until it cries out for theology. The only way to reach this point at which we become aware of our need for prayer, for hope, for stories of people who have been liberated, is to go deeply enough into our own sociohistorical context. The theologian will discover the inner necessity of theology in a given situation and its potential for unfolding theological meaning. We have to reach this point of no return where we will know anew that we do need God. This is the basis of doing theology, but the only way to come to this point is worldly analysis of our situation.

The third step is meditation. The verb is "to remember." We read the Bible out of our thirst for justice. We search in scripture and tradition for help. In what sense does the tradition help us? If we don't find an answer, we look for those parts of the tradition which at least speak to our despair. The literary form now is exegesis and the goal is to "remember" ourselves; to remember that we are members and children of Life and not of Death. We remember the resurrection.

The fourth step is a renewed praxis. What the theologian should learn here is to dream and to hope. Our imagination has been freed from original sinful bondages, and we are empowered to imagine alternative institutions. We become agents of change. Prayer and action become our doing. The literary form is now the creative envisioning. We find new language. Only this last step discloses the text and makes us not only into readers but into "writers" of the Bible. We say to each other "take up your bed and walk," which is a necessary step in any liberation theology.

These four steps from praxis to analysis to meditation to renewed praxis have an irreversible dynamic. In this sense the Spirit who moves in all these phases transcends where we are and who we are.

PART I
The Dispossessed

CHAPTER ONE

Street People in the U.S.A.

Yesterday evening at half past twelve we found an old man under an arch of the Brooklyn Bridge, lying on a pile of rags, wrapped up in a blanket. With difficulty he raised his head when we passed by and nodded to greet us. "How are you tonight?" asked my woman friend who is on the staff of a church relief program for the homeless. The aged black man complained of headaches. We asked whether he wanted a hot supper and went back to our delivery van with its soup kettle, bread and butter, and clothes. I gave him a lunch box. "I am Dorothee," I said. "What's your name?" "Greg," he murmured and sipped the soup in little gulps. It was a wonderfully mild evening in early spring, but today, as I write this, rain is pouring down from the sky. I think of Greg under the arch of the bridge. He may be entering his sixties. His blanket seemed relatively sturdy to me, but if it is soaked through from below. . . .

At the beginning of 1990, a sixty-year-old man was found dead in Chicago under an abandoned trailer in an open field. A few hundred steps from the place where he died were fifteen hundred warm, heated, vacant apartments with running water.

In New York there are seventy-five thousand homeless street people, unemployed, many of them sick from alcohol or addicted to drugs, physically handicapped, mentally deranged, or belonging to the very last category: homeless and sick with AIDS. "You don't need to be afraid," another said to me, peering out of his cardboard box. "We aren't criminals. We don't steal; we don't burglarize; we are only . . . homeless." Melman with the friendly brown eyes lies in his crate.

3

"You look like Noah in his ark," came to my mind, and he laughed. "I know what the Flood is." My woman friend told me of a young man who usually stayed next to Melman. Meanwhile, we are at a street corner where heat streams out of an office building. The boy did not eat, did not drink, and spoke with no one. Melman, the fatherly one, kept him alive. For a few days he was away, and he seemed to be better. "Why doesn't he speak?" I ask Noah in the ark. "He seems depressed," he answered—and stupidly it occurred to me to ask why. He always knew what the boy needed, a toothbrush, a few socks, a rainproof parka. Our relief group writes such requests down on a slip of paper with name, shoe size, and shirt size. "We'll see what we can do," they say, "that is, by next week, Friday night."

The purpose of these visits on the street is not only to bring hot chocolate, lunch boxes, bars of soap, and clothing to the poor. It is important to speak with them—at least as important for us as for them. We stand in front, shake hands, chat, ask questions, and embrace. We mainly meet men; most homeless women go to the homeless shelters, which one man described to me as stinking, loud, and over-supervised. The women are afraid of being raped by the street people. Among the forty people we encountered were two women, a young girl, and a Puerto Rican woman who wanders about with her friend. She has been on the street for six months and in a few minutes finishes three paper cups of hot chocolate. She clings to her friend. What will she do, I ask myself, when he cuts out? Another woman, far advanced in pregnancy, says that in three weeks it will be "her turn." She will visit a clinic, but what will become of the child is unclear.

Among the three million Americans who are homeless, there are a half million children. If the present trend continues, eighteen million people in the United States will be homeless in the year 2003. Even now, half of all the poor spend half of their income to pay their rent.

Since the beginning of the 1980s, the housing calamity has become greater and greater. More prosperity and more hunger are the economic quintessence of the Reagan-Bush era. Twenty percent of the rich are aided by tax relief. Rent subsidies and state-owned apartments—too few anyway— were systematically reduced. The victims of these economic decisions lie on the streets today. The middle class moved to the outlying suburbs. Houses in the cities decayed. Owners did not repair them anymore since only poor persons lived there anyway. Since the seventies there has been a trend of the rich young successful returning to the inner city. Houses are purchased; inhabitants are thrown out; whole blocks are snapped up and replaced. Stylish condominium apartments with enormous prices arise where pensioners, single women with children, and many nonwhites previously lived. Rental apartments are becoming increasingly scarce; publicly financed apartments have not been built since the beginning of the Reagan era. Thus the pauperization of the cities grows along with the "gentrification."

What the government builds for the poor are urgently needed prisons and, most recently, homeless shelters to make this third world invisible in the midst of the splendid first. These shelters do not even represent an attempt at solving the problems. One part of the population is supposed to be isolated, uneducated, unemployable, sick, and torn between despair and rage. Youths who grow up here are described as devoid of any morality and without any feeling of self-esteem. One homeless person writes: "Their only college is the prison, and an early death on the street is their Social Security."

What should be done? A housing construction program with decent conditions and fair prices is not in sight. There is charitable relief from churches and synagogues anxious that the poorest among the homeless receive at least occasional assistance. There are tent cities and cardboard shelters, as in the time of the Great Depression; the only difference is that the economy flourishes today.

There are encouraging experiments in self-help and self-organization, occupation of houses, and detoxification programs, alongside educational programs that constantly fail.

There is a monthly journal, *Voices for and from the Streets*, but none of this changes anything in the continuing pauperization. The great American promise to give everyone a chance is broken a million times. An embittered Vietnam veteran living in a tent by the river expresses his relationship to the nation and to ardent nationalism this way: "Should I burn the flag? Hell no! I'd rather do like Bush and wrap myself in it. But I wouldn't do this to capture votes but because I'm freezing." The flag does not help him anymore. It blows proudly over the unbroken militarism and the obsession of this country with war, whether "Star Wars" or the war on drugs, a war that heals no one, least of all the victims of the system, who alone give a reading of the humanity of a society.

CHAPTER TWO

The Future of the Poor

God's future cannot be conceived without "God's favorite children," as the poor were called at the Latin American Bishops' Conference in Puebla (1979). What will happen to them in God's future? Will they become rich like us? Will they remain poor? And if so, in what sense? What does God have in mind?

For this work dedicated to Jürgen Moltmann ["God's Future—Future of the World"] I have more questions than answers. One of my main difficulties is that the poor are largely invisible for us living in the middle class of the rich world. In Hamburg, the city where I live, I do not know a poor family personally. In the United States I have good friends who live on welfare and hardly have any hope of ever finding work. Still my personal knowledge is limited. In my uncertainty toward the poor I see that things I regard as superfluous luxury are necessary for them and vice versa. Sometimes I have the impression that we are just now beginning to understand—after nearly five centuries of Protestantism—who the poor are, how far they are ahead of us, and what they can teach us. The principle of liberation theology, "The poor are our teachers," becomes more important to me every day. For example, the hope, pain, and perseverance of the people in Nicaragua or in South Africa put me to shame and make me stronger. For us Christians in the first world I hope that we will develop the theology of God's future on the basis of a better acquaintance with the poor. I see no other way to God's future. If we disregard the poor and keep ourselves apart from them, then we pursue—intentionally or unintentionally—a theology of the rich. May we learn more from the poor, perhaps even what we have to expect ourselves from a more just economic policy, namely, to become poorer.

Two years ago Ronald Reagan was addressed by reporters on the ever deteriorating situation of the poor in the United States. In his answer he avoided the word *poor* and spoke instead of the nonrich. This term shocked me, although I knew that the only foreign language that Reagan commands is the Orwellian. What does it mean, I asked myself, when someone no longer uses the word *poor?* Is it one of the dirty four-letter words that should not be used? The distortion of language signals a new political paradigm. Most importantly, it expresses a denial of reality: the poor are not even poor. There are no poor in the United States. There is also no hunger, as the president protested on another occasion: the people only have a special diet. Reality may not be seen and named. The most important media in the U.S. follow this scenario: the nonrich are invisible and are nonpersons. Speaking about the "nonrich" implies at the same time an attack on the dignity of the poor. What I call their spiritual reality has to be neutralized.

The word *poor* contains different connotations and dangerous remembrances of another form of life. In the Germanic languages *poor* is connected with "dear," "worthy of compassion," and "abandoned," as we know from colloquial expressions ("a poor fool," "a poor dog"). These terms correspond to a Judeo-Christian tradition of compassion, which can have no place anymore in the calculated social dismantling and deconstruction of the eighties. Already in 1981 the National Council of Churches declared programmatically in a "word to the churches" (Sept. 1981):

> The new administration demands a revision of our understanding that a government is responsible in principle for "furthering the common welfare." . . . The policy of the new administration aims not only at cutting social benefits but also denies that people have a right to them.

In recent years the United States has gradually attained a pre-Rooseveltian state concerning social welfare. The government no longer even makes the claim of advancing the whole society and has abandoned the national dream of a just society, a new Jerusalem without exploitation and slavery with its roots in Christianity and the Enlightenment. Since the beginning of the eighties, larger and larger portions of the population have been subjected to systematic pauperization. Amid the surplus that continues to mark the rich industrial nations, poverty and hunger are spreading in Europe and North America while food production is simultaneously reduced with subsidies from tax monies. But this growing minority must not become too visible; there are no poor, only some nonrich.

Without a doubt poverty and riches are extraordinarily relative ideas, which have very different meanings in different societies and times. To use them meaningfully, we must learn to think contextually, relationally, and postmaterialistically. These are methodological presuppositions that a discourse on the new poverty will hopefully fulfill. By "contextual" I mean the life context within which the calculated impoverishment takes place, for example, the difference between dismissed older women workers and young people who are generally excluded from the work experience. "Relational" means "standing in relation to": one cannot speak about the new poor and be silent about the rich. Therefore the charitable initiative of state relief programs is about as ingenious as trying to heal the gravely ill with pain pills. With "postmaterialist" I would like (cautiously) to call into question the conventional identification of work with wage-earning. Human dignity must be based on something other then wages. Human rights have to be redefined, going beyond the middle-class framework of freedom of religion, press, and assembly.

These preliminary reflections are necessary to save ourselves from a relativism that levels everything. "What does poor mean? Measured by Calcutta. . . ." This is cynical talk about both those dying of hunger in two-thirds of the world and the new poor in the rich world.

Let us start with the acknowledged basic needs of people. Food, health, education, housing, clothing, work, and communication are needs whose denial makes people "poor"; withholding them impoverishes or destroys. As everybody knows, there are "many ways of killing. One can stick a knife into someone's belly, deprive someone of bread, not heal someone of a sickness, consign someone to a miserable dwelling, work to death, drive to suicide, send to war, and so forth. Very little of this is prohibited in our state" (Bertolt Brecht, *Gesammelte Werke* 12:466). In these notes of Brecht, the dignity of the person is assumed. The comparison with Calcutta is entirely inappropriate for the homeless communities on the edge of our mass cities. The questions we really have to raise are: When is poverty degrading? Under what conditions does it destroy the dignity of the person?

Not every form of poverty has this destructive quality. At the beginning of November 1984, president-elect Daniel Ortega gave a speech in Nicaragua in which he made clear to his hearers the great hardship of the war and the threat of destruction by the United States. He said he had nothing to promise other than "beans, rice, and human dignity." One of the great fascinations of Nicaragua for the visitor from the rich world is that there is extreme poverty everywhere, but in most cases poverty is not degrading—above all because it is a collective fate, not the punishment of individual people. A third of Managua's population lives in the shacks of the poor, often constructed out of sheet metal, wood, and a few stones. These are "slums" but are not comparable with those I have seen in Mexico City, Santiago de Chile, or Buenos Aires. In the new quarter of El Retiro, for example, all the huts have electricity, garbage is not strewn on the mud paths, water is distributed to the whole region, and most people wear shoes. "What does the revolution mean for you?" I asked a young woman and mother of six children on the outskirts of the city of Managua. "My children will learn something," she said, and before the one-room hut made of a little wood and sheet metal a beautiful, barefoot child declared, with an arrogance that five-year-olds sometimes have, that later she would study and become a doctor.

There are forms of poverty that do not destroy the dignity of people. Christian tradition can be understood only if we start with this possibility. Why are the forms of the new pauperization appearing among us? Why is our poverty of the elderly, women, large families, unemployed, and unemployable so different and so destructive? Under what social and psycho-social conditions does poverty destroy the dignity of the person? The new poverty is humiliating. There are many reports of unemployed who hide their dismissal from neighbors and often from their own families, who pretend to ride to work in the morning on the bus and return in the evening because they cannot endure the humiliation and social exclusion. They find themselves completely dependent on the arbitrariness of those who decide over the destruction of jobs through new technologies. The poor lack sovereignty to relate to life, to make use of relationships with other people, and to develop playful elements in their own lives. This can go so far that the simplest questions are not raised by the poor, such as the question, "What does that cost?" Stories like the one of the woman living alone who was talked into buying a kilo of coffee per week by an agent and did not know how to avoid the trap are not rare. The dependence of the poor destroys their mobility and curiosity. The uncertainty of life expands immediately. Subjective self-degradation is joined to the objective subjugation to social controls. In fact, poverty is a dirty word better left unmentioned, and this consciousness fits the poor.

Their children learn it on entering school. I recall a meeting of parents in the first year of high school. The woman teacher said cheerfully, "If something happens, you can call me. Perhaps we should all exchange our telephone numbers." I thought nothing of this myself, but beside me sat an intimidated mother who asked: "Do we have to have a telephone?" She was rattled by a familiarity, mobility, and style of communication strange to her. She was afraid of doing something wrong and spoke, if at all, only to me. Half a year later her child was out of school. I relate this example to point to a phenomenon of the new poverty, the subjective consciousness of having no rights. The principle of need is so eroded in social welfare that the legal claims of those affected have become the discretionary decisions of the bureaucracy. Dependence increases and degradation turns into self-degradation. The schoolchild for whose parents the announced class trip is too expensive stays away and withdraws, and the imposed exclusion from the local community and the community of life is internalized in many small steps.

The poor are separated from society. This happens in legislative measures, which entail social degradation, isolation, and lack of cultural or political participation. The rich do not want to endure the sight of the poor. From an account in the *New York Times* I learned that a growing number of rich villages in the United States are delimiting themselves from the rest. There is an architecture of the "rich in fear" who build armed houses: little castles with high hedges, biting dogs, and alarm systems. These walled villages in America are usually not near places with high criminality. Nevertheless, the rich's fear of the poor is already so great that electronic security zones and armed guards are necessary. The ancient idea of the city, the polis in which free citizens live together, is abandoned in favor of an architecture of apartheid that makes the poor invisible. They are nonpersons, Reagan's denial of their reality only expresses the consciousness of his class. There are no poor.

In South Africa the overwhelming majority of white youths grow up in complete cultural apartheid. They do not know their own country; they know nothing about the water supply and electricity in townships like Soweto. The working conditions of the nonwhites are entirely unknown to them. This intellectual and cultural apartheid is not just an invention of South African racists; it is fundamental to the whole culture of the rich. For example, there are whole theologies and institutions founded on them, in which the poor are not even present but remain invisible. The rich world needs more and more walls to entrench itself against the poor, and more and more weapons to secure itself against them. The separation of the poor, making them invisible, is ideologically necessary. Therefore Reagan's contortions of language are not an accident. The refuse, the increasing marginalization of whole new generations of poor, is veiled as much as possible.

In the summer of 1984 the German Trade Union Federation (DGB) presented a study on the separation of the unemployed. Among other conclusions the study stated that the "new poverty" among the unemployed is a calculated consequence of social retrenchment. At the same time as the DGB study on the new poverty, a pastoral letter of the French bishops was published on the same theme. "There is hunger today in France," this declaration begins. Hunger is not a marginal phenomenon or a kind of "accident" in an otherwise flourishing economic order, but rather the reality of 600,000 to 1,000,000 very normal French people in an economic system that intensively applies the latest technologies and puts up with the unemployed. This political and economic development is safeguarded by new ideologies propagated in the increasingly popular philosophical school of the Nouvelle Droite, the New Right. Every week on glossy paper *Figaro* magazine popularizes the new "cult of the stronger," identifies the stronger, the beautiful, and the powerful as the better, and gives the rich a good conscience. Thus are the walls of ideological apartheid built up; the ideal of equality is demonized as "leveling" and "egalitarianism." The cult of the strong, which finds more and more adherents in the younger generation of students, is openly proclaimed as a "new paganism." Away at last with the remnants of a solidarity community of the strong and the weak! The poor are themselves guilty—this is the new ideology that is expressed in an anticlerical and pagan way by the French and in a fundamentalist and Christofascist fashion by Reagan. The dignity of the poor is in fact under attack.

In West Germany ideology limps somewhat behind, but the practical and bureaucratic administration of the poor is already perfect. Financial costs for the poor are shifted from the nation to the states and communities in order to work toward their isolation and decentralization. Social problems are to remain depoliticized. The poor, the unemployed, and those living without prospect for change must be isolated from one another. The transfer of authority serves the political incapacitation of those forced to the edge. At a round of talks between economic leaders and representatives of German Protestantism, the church's role in the economy was recently formulated in cynical openness. The church should motivate the employees for meaningless work and outfit them with a new working morale. The unemployed should be kept quiet by pointing to the "meaning of life." This manner of avoiding the problem of the new poverty is not only cynical but also blind to reality. I cannot imagine that the members of the power elite actually want to live as the ideology of wealth prescribes: in armed houses, behind walls in private settlements, equipped with fallout shelters and protected by paid guards who stop approaching intruders. A society that isolates the poor and renounces community solidarity between the strong and the weak, the employed and the unemployed, the childless and those with large families must also refuse the democratic form of political life. Democracy does not function under the presuppositions of social Darwinism but presupposes cooperative thinking, mutual responsibility, a *bonum commune*. The cancellation of this community and mutual dependence represents the war of the rich against the poor. War in the ideology of the new right becomes the vision of life: one always has to prepare for war as the natural reality. The condition of pauperization into which the elite of the rich world plunge the poorest in the third world cannot be maintained without war and violence. The undeclared war of the richest land on earth against one of the poorest should have made that clear even to the most naive defenders of Western ideologies.

The rich destroy not only the human dignity of the poor but also their own. They have chained their dignity to possessions and to the violent expedients bound up with possessions. Not every form of poverty destroys human dignity, but every form of wealth that remains unrelated to the dependent and has to isolate itself behind apartheid walls is a self-destruction of the human dignity of the rich. A rich person

entering the kingdom of heaven is as likely as a camel pass-
ing through the eye of a needle.

In the discussion of poverty and riches the Christian tradition has something to offer that is in danger of being forgotten today. Christian tradition does not start from the
assumption that all people are capitalists, some successful
(i.e., rich) and others unsuccessful and handicapped (i.e.,
poor). This assumption is obvious in our culture, and the dignity of the poor—the reason why Jesus called them blessed—
is absolutely unintelligible. However, it is a materialist
superstition to assume that every form of poverty destroys
our dignity and is to be avoided at any price. As long as we
consider the poor under the dominant point of view, namely,
as handicapped capitalists, we understand nothing. The dignity of the poor lies in their being, not in their having and not
having; the destruction of their dignity is the destruction of
their solidarity with one another and their vision together.

I have identified the criteria that make poverty destructive
and self-destructive: humiliation, shame, isolation, and mean-
inglessness. Still that does not define the poor always and
everywhere. The Bible is a committed adversary to all fatalism,
to every description of human reality as ending fatefully.
Against the idea that "because you are poor, you will die earlier," it insists that "because you are rich, you have never lived."
The gospel is full of woes against the rich and beatitudes for
the poor. It promises liberation and fullness of life to the hungry, those deprived of rights, and the artificially impoverished.
Two kinds of poverty can be distinguished within the Christian
tradition: the forced pauperization inflicted upon people, what
is called "absolute poverty" by the economists, and the voluntarily chosen poverty in which people postpone their material
needs and gain freedom from one another through simplicity
and frugality. The great woman of American Catholicism,
Dorothy Day (1897–1980), a modern saint, is for me the clearest example of such voluntarily chosen poverty. The Catholic
Worker movement founded by her brings together voluntary
poverty with consistent nonviolence and resistance to militarism.

The promise of the gospel is not that everyone is to become like the rich. The ideal is not the millionaire and his
generals but rather little people, women, and children who
were promised "life in abundance" physically, intellectually,
and mentally in a culture of sharing, where five loaves of
bread and two fish are enough to divide among five thousand people.

The surprising miracle stories in the Gospels can give us
distance from ourselves (and the capitalist in us) and provide
a better understanding of the role of the poor. One principle
of the theology of liberation, which one can also call a theology of the poor, is that the poor are teachers who draw our
attention to life. What do the poor teach us? They wait for
miracles. They need miracles whereas for the rich miracles
are only superstition, illusion, and flight from reality. The
poor need a miracle: a repealing of the laws of reality that
whoever falls will be pushed further, that the strong are vic-
torious over the weak and do violence to them. They need the
miracle that solidarity is stronger than the structural violence
of the powerful. The poor do not need reforms, relief programs, and placebos; they need the miracle whose core is redistribution. A new redistribution of work hours, income,
and free time according to the principle of need—this is a
hope without which the poor cannot preserve their dignity.
In this sense the Sandinista revolution that redistributed land,
food, health, and education was a miracle story in which the
seemingly impossible became possible. "All things are possible to the one who believes," says Jesus. In his message "believing" in miracles means sharing in them and doing them.

The promise of God's future in such a solidarity culture is
an invitation to struggle, advocacy for the victims, and compassion. People who are drawn to the side of the poor come
into contact with the foundation of all life. The Bible declares
that God encounters them in the poor. With this step from
unconsciousness to consciousness, from apathetic hopelessness regarding one's fate to faith in the liberating God of the
poor, the quality of poverty also changes because one's relationship to it changes. If poor people are only handicapped

capitalists, their relationship to poverty cannot change. They will play the lottery again and wait for chance employment and an individual solution to a social problem. In the future they will be ashamed of poverty and regard isolation as natural. They will internalize the culture of apartheid and define their own dignity capitalistically in possessions and achievements. But if they become conscious of their situation, their relation to themselves changes. Seen quantitatively, their poverty can become greater, since struggle and compassion demand sacrifice. It can also become less, since the struggle and the compassion already represent a better distribution of goods. However, the forced, imposed poverty is no longer the same in the two cases. It if adopts the features of voluntary poverty, the reality of freedom in poverty shines forth. It becomes God's poverty as it was for Jesus, Francis, Oscar Romero, and many others. In this way the poor become involved in the struggle for liberation. What now sounds like a dream—the consciousness of the unconscious—has its models in the third world. The poor have already united; liberation conflicts are taking place; the culture of apathy and degrading silence is overcome; rice, beans, and human dignity are shared. Why should we not also have a trade union of persons excluded from the working life? a new solidarity between those who still have work and those whose dignity is threatened by the denial of the human right to work? a movement for peace that understands the marginalization and degradation of the poor as part of the merciless war that the first world wages against two-thirds of the human family, against nature, and against itself? "Why will you die?" asked the prophet Ezekiel (33:11). Why indeed?

The future of God is the future of the poor. Without them there will be no future for the Christian God. God will make the poor "rich," but in the sense that we use the word in the German hymn: "Remember Christ in heaven/how he made us rich and blessed." God will make them rich in being, not in having; rich in relationship, not in possessions; rich in God, if we may speak this way, as poor Jesus, St. Francis and St. Clare, Dorothy Day, and many others were. No, we must say *are*.

CHAPTER THREE

Jesus and Women's Self-Acceptance

Every woman who tries to be a Christian today must ask herself how she can relate her gender and her membership in the community of believers. Sickened by the rule of men in the church, does she not have to turn her back on Christianity? Indeed, there is an old tradition of disdain and even hatred for women that has not been overcome and is nourished by the most threadbare theological pretexts, which still flourish beneath a sham liberalism. Even the worship of masculine values, for example, the adoration of power at any price, knowledge and research even at the cost of the fabric of life, conquest and subjugation as the main forms of associating with one another—all this masculine splendor has its roots in the religiously practiced humiliation and contempt of nature and women. Today the most sensitive and alert women often feel homeless in Christianity and forced out of churches. In their deep insecurity some have begun struggling with the conflict. For twenty years this struggle has been pursued under the heading "feminist theology," and for ten years even in a theologically very undeveloped country like Germany. One of the central motifs of this theology is the mutual relationship between Jesus and women.

The History of Christianity Between Open Hatred of Women and Liberating Deliverance from the Oldest Injustices

I begin with a quotation from Teresa of Avila, that Spanish woman and mystic who fought for religious freedom against an overwhelmingly one-sided society of men and church of men. In Spain at that time women were forbidden to learn to read and write, to read the Bible, or to practice the art of meditation. For women it was enough to learn knitting and to pray the Our Father and the Ave Maria! Many letters of Teresa have not been released for publication over the centuries. "Bold" statements in the manuscripts of her books and letters are nearly illegible, particularly where she turned sharply against discrimination against women. Nevertheless, she appealed to Jesus' attitude toward women. In one dialogue with Christ, which the censor made almost unreadable and which was missing for a long time from many editions of her writings, she said: "When you were in this world, far from despising women, you encountered them with great kindness. You found greater love and more faith among them than among men. When I look at our world today, it is unjust that people with virtuous and strong minds are scorned only because they are women."[1]

The whole ambiguity of our theme is set forth in these sentences. Jesus, the founder of the Christian religion, found "greater love and more faith" among women, but they are despised by the institution solely because they're women. This contradiction pervades the entire history of Christianity but appears most clearly in the founding document itself, the New Testament. This book, written only by men, as far as we know, is deeply marked by the patriarchy of the ancient world. We find both underestimation of women and open hatred of women, on the one hand, and liberating deliverance from the oldest injustice, which Jesus and the original Jesus movement represent, on the other.

The Jesus movement was a group of female and male friends who followed the little man from Nazareth. Many had no fixed dwelling and had abandoned their traditional family bonds. The women who followed him through the land had withdrawn from the patriarchal marriage order and its supervision. Many were already divorced or abandoned by their husbands. We can best imagine these conditions if we think of the vast slums of Latin America, for

example, where the poorest of the poor are women. When
the New Testament speaks on almost every page about the
sick, we must think here of sick women, blind, paralyzed,
and seared by misery. Many were psychically sick, or possessed by demons, as the New Testament says. The Jesus
movement offered hope for these sufferers. They were
healed and began to heal others. They heard the good news
of liberation and passed it on. They were filled, and they
shared the little they had.

The Jesus movement lived in conflict with its society. Jesus
expected the reversal of all social oppositions through God's
intervention, and this expectation—"the kingdom of God is
at hand"—characterized the movement. All those who were
outsiders according to the norms of society and held to be
"impure" according to the law—the poor, the landless, public sinners, tax collectors, and women—were accepted here.
"The last will be first" is a keynote permeating the whole
message of Jesus. Who are these "last"? We could think of
farmers overcome by debt, expelled from their leased land,
and deprived of their rights. But even below them, regarded
as religiously inferior and cultically impure, stood women.
Being a woman was the last of all!

The Restoration of the Image of God in Women
through the Jesus Movement

One of the most beautiful stories in the New Testament con-
cerns a woman who had a flow of blood for twelve years.
She was socially isolated because according to ancient no-
tions, menstruation and bleeding women's diseases were
deemed dangerous for the environment. Objects touched by
such women became unclean. They could not join in the
Passover sacrifice. Menstruation, women's diseases, and lep-
rosy were considered similar problems. Plinius described the
general attitude toward such sicknesses. "Cider that comes
too near people in this condition becomes sour. . . . Garden
plants dry up, and the fruits of the tree from which they eat

fall off. . . . Rust immediately befalls brass and iron, just as malicious gossip attacks the air. . . ."[2]

A woman who "had endured much under many physicians, and had spent all that she had; and she was no better, but rather grew worse" (Mark 5:26) approached Jesus and touched him. "She had heard about Jesus, and came up behind him in the crowd and touched his cloak, for she said, 'If I but touch his clothes, I will be made well.'" As in most accounts of healing the sick, it is the ill person, here the shunned woman, who creates the relationship with Jesus, who "touches" him and trusts his strength. The mystery of Jesus is the power, the dynamis of God, which is in him and is released in the encounter with others. Healing is not possible "in and of itself" through Jesus, the miracle-worker, the superman, but in mutual relationship.[3] Jesus had touched the woman's heart; therefore she wanted to take hold of his cloak.

Once after a lecture I experienced something very beautiful. An elderly woman came to me and embraced me saying, "You touched me, and I want to touch you." I do not know whether that was a healing, but in any case a power was at work, something of the life-giving power, the *dynamis*, that the woman with the flow of blood aroused in Jesus.

Masculine concepts of competition and sovereignty lead interpreters to think that Jesus had a monopoly on this power. Jesus was not an eccentric; he did not "possess" God and "hold" power in the relationship as property. It was the faith of this despised, injured woman that made her whole. In this touching and letting ourselves be touched, we experience the power of God. We must regard the miracle narratives as stories of the love that lives in the world and liberates. We rightly understand the accounts when we remember Jesus' summons to his female and male disciples to heal the sick themselves, to drive out demons, to feed the hungry, and to proclaim the good news. The authoritarian God from above cannot really help us, but rather the gentle God, who is expressed in different and changing ways in relations among sisters and brothers. Hence Jesus and the Jesus movement had to come into conflict with hierarchical, patriarchal thinking. The Spirit of God cannot govern according to sexual characteristics, and the oldest injustice cannot continue in the reign announced by Jesus.

Theologically expressed, the image of God in women, which patriarchy seeks to destroy, was restored in the Jesus movement. The woman has an unrestricted share in the mystery of life and in God. She was not excluded as a woman from experiences with Jesus. She had a place in the story of the great healings that occurred in the Jesus movement. The blind see and those enslaved by their own powerlessness are touched, so that as men and women they experience God's spirit and do the work of God. Giving sight to the blind, making peace, and exorcising demons happens today when women in Greenham Common, In Hunsrück before nuclear weapons, or before the Pentagon expel militarism, the greatest demon that possesses us.

The Reaction of Patriarchy
to Jesus' Commandment of Equality

The theme "Jesus and Women" not only means that Jesus was not a sexist and a macho, that there is not a single negative word from him about women, that he made them disciples, and that he healed them from the anxiety of being only a woman, a weak, second-rate being! It also means that these Jesus women received courage and strength to oppose the generally accepted values of racism, exclusivity, structural injustice, and patriarchy. Women were not marginal figures in the Jesus movement but apostles, prophetesses, and missionaries.[4] In Christ all are one and of equal birth. "There is no longer Jew or Greek, there is no longer slave or free, there is no longer male or female; for all of you are one in Christ Jesus!" said Paul in the Letter to the Galatians (3:28). Class injustice, religious exclusivity, and the patriarchal conditions of rule were superseded in principle in the Jesus movement. People accepted Jesus as the liberator from these distortions and structures of authority. They saw him as the envoy of

God who brings true life, not only new advantages for one-half of humanity. They called him the Christ.

Alongside the confession of Peter to this Christ, which is often celebrated as unique by tradition, there is the Messiah confession of Martha of Bethany, who according to the Gospel of John confesses her faith in the words: "Yes, Lord, I believe that you are the Messiah, the Son of God, the one who is coming into the world" (John 11:27). Peter and Martha were the first who confessed the Redeemer. However, thirty years after Paul and in glaring contradiction to his gospel of freedom—"There is no longer slave or free, male or female"—it says very differently in the First Letter to Timothy, written by a pupil of Paul: "I permit no woman to teach or to have authority over a man; she is to keep silent. For Adam was formed first, then Eve; and Adam was not deceived, but the woman was deceived and became a transgressor. Yet she will be saved through childbearing, provided they [i.e., Christian women] continue in faith and love and holiness, with modesty" (1 Tim. 2:12–15).

The reaction of patriarchy to the primitive Christian feminism of Jesus is reflected in these catastrophically portentous words. As a matter of fact, women taught in the churches, the resurrected Christ first appeared to women, and women knew that the discipleship of Christ makes people free, not the fulfillment of a sexual role. These words from 1 Timothy are false and lying words; they garnish a claim of rule with a precarious, self-righteous interpretation of the story of the banishment from paradise—as though Adam were innocent! They also practice treachery on what Paul emphasizes theologically, that people are not rescued by "Children's Crusades" (as in 1212), asceticism, or other good works, but by faith in the person and message of Christ! If early Catholicism had been right here with its patriarchal fear of teaching, thinking, independent women, Christianity would have been no more than an ideology of subordination; then the penis would justify and not the truth!

The New Testament contains contradictions that cannot be reconciled by glossing over them. The two lines shown here—liberation from the powerlessness and slavery of sin, healing, and deliverance on the one hand and stabilization of repression on the other—cannot be abolished from the world. Martin Luther knew that we need criteria to judge the Bible. The question for him was whether the scripture "proclaims Christ" or not. What happens when it concentrates on mere patriarchy, as in the First Letter to Timothy? Then the men protecting their rule deny the liberating Christ. They hold his truth captive under the cover of a patriarchy hostile to the Spirit. That is the criticism and questioning of feminist theology regarding patriarchal thinking and its sexist praxis.

The Tears of Mary Magdalene in the Resurrection Narrative

The clearest sign of what was intended in primitive Christianity is found in the Easter narratives of the New Testament. Women persevered with Jesus in his suffering and were witnesses of the empty tomb and the resurrection.

Mark, the oldest Gospel, declares that women were the first witnesses to the basic facts of Jesus' life. The death, burial, and resurrection were not made known to us by those who ran away and hid, that is, the men, but by those present, the women. The most important figure in the Jesus movement, which rejoiced in women, was Mary Magdalene. Like the entire community, she fell into deep despair after Jesus' execution. In the night after the burial, she ran to Jesus' grave and saw that the stone that had blocked the vault of the tomb was missing. In desperation she complained to others that the body had disappeared. She was more courageous than the men, since she sought Jesus at the tomb, in the public shunned by men.

The Romans crucified the Jew Jesus because he incited the people to resistance against Rome.[5] He preached about the God of Israel, the only king of the world, who grants a brief time to political rulers for their regime of violence contemptuous of human beings. The Romans publicly crucified such disturbers of their rule. One could not even weep publicly over the death of a crucified person. Tacitus reports the Roman practice regarding political executions: "Not even women were spared from trials. Since they could not be charged with intentionally seizing power in the state, they were accused on account of their tears. The elderly Vitia, the mother of Fufius Geminus, was killed because she cried at the execution of her son." Mary's tears and her despair are mentioned again and again in the narrative of the Gospel of John. Everyone knew that crying was dangerous in this situation.

Everyone also knew what the empty tomb of a crucified person meant. The Roman occupying power or its accomplices let the corpse disappear to prevent the grave from becoming a center of resistance and meeting place for Jesus' followers. (The funerals of the murdered South Africans have been places of public resistance against the white apartheid government.)

The way to the graves of the murdered is the way of Mary Magdalene:

> But Mary stood weeping outside the tomb. As she wept, she bent over to look into the tomb; and she saw two angels in white, sitting where the body of Jesus had been lying, one at the head and the other at the feet. They said to her, "Woman, why are you weeping?" She said to them, "They have taken away my Lord, and I do not know where they have laid him." When she had said this, she turned around and saw Jesus standing there, but she did not know that it was Jesus. Jesus said to her, "Woman, why are you weeping? Whom are you looking for?" Supposing him to be the gardener, she said to him, "Sir, if you have carried him away, tell me where you have laid him, and I will take him away."
>
> (John 20:11–15)

In this first text of the resurrection narratives in the Gospel of John, the crying of Mary Magdalene is the focus of interest. The text relates her grief and her movements very precisely. She sought Jesus' corpse; she sought the person who had shown her where life and hope could be found in the world. The angels at Jesus' tomb did not say, "Be quiet, stop crying!" They asked, "Why are you weeping?" Jesus did not say to Mary Magdalene, "Be quiet, stop your endless lamentation and wailing!" He asked her, "Woman, why are you weeping?"

Jesus Was a Feminist

We seek justice; we seek peace. We women seek a future for coming generations that is not poisoned. We yearn for life; we yearn for light. We seek God. Mary Magdalene was called the "apostle of the apostles" because she called men to life and resurrection, the men who had become despondent.

In primitive Christianity there was a passionate controversy over whether Peter or Mary Magdalene was the first witness of the resurrection. Both still had apostolic authority in several communities in the third and fourth centuries. Many communities simply acknowledged the claim of women to leadership. Gradually Jesus' hope for women, his humanity, disappeared from the church. We could speak of a "progressive patriarchalization of ecclesiastical office." The just traditions of the original Jesus movement, which were friendly to women and thus to humanity, have not prevailed in the church. Early Catholicism arose with orthodoxy and heresy defined and imposed in the interest of the rule of men. The charisma, the genuine calling by the Spirit, was thrust aside by the office. The egalitarian gospel—"Call no one master; call no one father"—was superseded by the hierarchy.

Nevertheless, this hierarchy holding women to be eternally and spiritually inferior did not succeed in completely extinguishing the Spirit. Jesus' impact was too strong. The message of those who, with the courage to remain by the one tortured to death, had the confidence to touch him and first understood that Christ was not killed—this power of faith sounded a bell of freedom reminding people that they were created as men and women, not as slaves and objects, in the likeness of the God who is our Father and Mother. The gospel of the liberation of humanity from sin and powerlessness, from fear and submissiveness under the domination of men, cannot be neatly trimmed to size either by the white race, by the rich, or by men who regard only themselves as people. Jesus had a greater freedom to offer than the freedom known to men. In today's language, he was a feminist. His transcendence surpassed men's dream of domination. His God was different; his God could not exist without justice and love. The question of love is a question of trust. Love is a light that never goes out, a light of acceptance and new creation.

Notes

1. J. Kotschner, ed., *Der Weg zum Quell. Teresa von Avila* (Düsseldorf, 1982), 18.

2. Cf. Luise Schottroff, "Frauen in der Nachfolge Jesu in neutestamentlicher Zeit," in *Frauen in der Bibel*, vol. 2 of *Traditionen der Befreiung*, ed. W. Schottroff and W. Stegemann (Munich, 1980), 106.

3. Cf. Carter Heyward, *The Redemption of God: A Theology of Mutual Relation* (Lanham, Md.: University Press of America, 1982), 46.

4. Cf. Elisabeth Schüssler-Fiorenza, "Der Beitrag der Frau zur urchristlichen Bewegung. Kritische Überlegungen zur Rekonstruktion urchristlicher Geschichte," in Schottroff and Stegemann, *Frauen in der Bibel*, 82.

5. Cf. Luise Schottroff, Dorothee Soelle, and Bärbel von Wartenberg, *Das Kreuz, Baum des Lebens* (Stuttgart, 1987), 10, 43.

PART II
Vision

CHAPTER FOUR

People Without Vision Perish

Vision

Where there is no vision, the people perish:
but he that keepeth the law, happy is he.
(Prov. 29:18, KJV)

"Where there is no vision . . ."—I recall how this biblical expression from an English translation of the Bible encountered me one day and lured me into meditation. The idea of "vision" was rather strange to me from the German vernacular. When someone asked me in the United States what my vision was, I stammered. Slowly I learned that this word in North America belongs to the great inheritance of liberation history. The vision of another land was the answer to the geopolitical, confessional, and the feudal-state narrowness and dependence of ancient Europe. Vision involves freedom, a greater freedom than now given. Visions are pictures "of a land where it will be easier to be good," proclaimed a great pacifist visionary of our century, Dorothy Day, cofounder of the Catholic Worker movement.

Where there is no prophecy [or revelation],
the people cast off restraint.   (NRSV)

"Revelation," "vision," and "prophecy" convey the voice of the prophets, who together with the law constituted the canon of the Hebrew Bible at that time. Thus vision and law cannot be understood as oppositions in which yogis and commissars face one another uncomprehendingly, with one group representing the visionary world of dreams and the other the world of real possibility. Rather, vision and Torah belong together in the Bible. Martin Buber emphasized again and again that the translation "law" for the Jewish Torah represents a falsification, a subjugation of Hebrew thought to Greek norms and ideas. In the Hebrew Bible Torah means more than the objective law, more than the legal constitution or collection of rules. Torah means direction, guidance, reference, advice, and instruction. God is not the lawgiver but the teacher. "Your eyes shall see your Teacher," exclaims Isaiah (30:20), referring to the people. The psalmist says, "Teach me your way, O Lord" (Ps. 27:11). In this sense law and vision complement one another. Instruction in the just life is renewed and remembered in the pictures of true life. Both primitive concepts are strictly focused on praxis. Vision is action-oriented, not a blessed contemplation of eternity. If we believe we can live without vision, we agree to a spiritual impoverishment that endangers life. Kierkegaard once spoke of the "base persecutions of mediocrity." Believing that visions are superfluous and pragmatism is enough is a sign of a self-satisfied mediocrity blind to danger and insensitive to pain.

With the Native Americans of the great prairie and the medicine wheel, we can ask: What pragmatism is this, the pragmatism of the mouse? Native Americans call a kind of one-dimensionality the "view of the mouse." They develop a philosophy of wholeness. The four directions are coordinated with four colors, four animals, and the four great forces in the person. To become whole we must learn to go in all four directions: to the North, whose sacred animal is the buffalo, embodying wisdom; to the South, which is represented by the mouse, typifying trust and innocence; to the West, directing our view inward under the sign of the bear; and to the East, which is defined by the sign of the eagle, symbolizing enlightenment, where we see things clearly and from afar.

I fear that with us the perspective of the mouse dominates the everyday life of many people, above all women, who have locked themselves in a mouselike existence. Nearness to all life and intimacy are the positive sides of this "gift of the South." Still the mouse is too close to the ground and too nearsighted to notice anything that it cannot touch with its moustache. Those who advance only in the direction of the mouse and lose sight of the great circle of the medicine wheel separate themselves from the wisdom of the buffalo, the illumination of the eagle, and the inward view that the bear can teach us. Growing holistically in all four directions, setting out on the way, and fulfilling the harmony of the great medicine wheel comprise the nature of the whole person who journeys the four great ways. Vision is manifest here.

In personal relations we miss one another when we do not know the vision of the other person or when we think we can forgo this knowledge. We know very little about one another when we do not share together the vision of life that supports us. We need pictures: of houses and cities where we live, of work, and of the relationships of people with one another. If we do not dare to dream together anymore, isolate our desires, and hide ashamed, we live in a suffocating gloominess or hollowness. It is as though we refuse to come to know the angel behind a person, as though our indifference is so great that we can content ourselves with the outside view of the mere present. Loving a person always means sensing the vision of the other. The community of love is shared vision.

Jesus called the reign of God the greatest vision, without which every other vision would be too small. This reign of God is within us (Luke 17:21) and should be first. The reign is already visible wherever references and relations are based on justice and love, and at the same time are hidden and powerless like the peace we seek.

Since the beginning of the eighties one thought has pressed me ever more preemptively; it expresses the death mania and desire for killing of our rich industrial society. My feeling is that we are living in war, even now. Perhaps we have lost all four directions. Daily we exterminate one of our fellow creatures, a plant or animal species, contrary to the natural foundations of life. Every day at least forty thousand persons die of hunger in the economic war between the rich and the poor. Day after day we perfect the war against ourselves by using our money, our raw materials, and our intelligence to prepare war. Not only is outer space militarized, but also the inner space of the soul has become a land occupied by threats and potential violence.

Justice, peace, and the preservation of creation are invoked by the ecumenical movement of Christians as a "conciliar process" against this war, but the forces of war are armed with vast technological power, and above all because they have engaged the most important productive force determining our life: science. If, as in the United States, fifty-one percent of the scientists and engineers work in military-related projects, that is, in the interest of death, then reconciliation with nature, the removal of hunger, and the peace that does not rest on military force will hardly be the goal of the power elite. It may sound exaggerated to some when I decry "war" against creation, the poor, and ourselves. However, this is not at all different from what the Christian tradition has expressed for two millennia with the central idea of sin, which is scarcely understood today.

Paul did not use the term *sin*, which appears forty-eight times in the Letter to the Romans, only to describe actual sinful acts. Rather, he thought of the much more comprehensive fact of the conditions of rule under which people live. Death is a power that governs even during life, involving and exploiting people in its violence. Paul calls this world power of death separating us from the origin of life "sin." It dominates the world, as the master rules his slaves and as a demon controls the possessed; it holds people captive (Rom. 7:23). Sin appears as a warlord who pays people their "wages" (Rom. 6:23), whose weapon is the person (6:13), and whose worldwide domination is death (Rom. 5:21). To all people God's will is manifestly justice, peace, and the integrity of creation, but the structure of death, which Paul calls the rule of sin, so enslaves people that they fail in attempting to live according to God's will. This warlord is at the same time the lawgiver of this world (7:23), which by its own self-dynamic is ordered to death.

Paul concretizes the world rule of sin in the dimensions of the Roman Empire. For the majority of people living at that time, this empire stood for brutal rule, economic plundering, and political oppression. The Roman Empire developed two instruments of rule, first its law, the *jus romanum*, regulating property relations, trade prices, subjugation of other peoples, and slavery, and second its military apparatus, which under the title *pax romana* guaranteed the stability of imperial rule. If Paul and the primitive Christian community understood sin as the essence of this legal and military system, which so enslaved people that they could not obey God, this is a hint of the present experience of Christians and post-Christians who like myself discern war as the reality dominating and poisoning everything.

Just as Paul could first recognize and name the power of sin from a viewpoint of inner freedom that in the Bible is called "faith," so our present experience of death and the prevalence of war, in which we live contrary to all things, is possible only with another force empowering us to resist. Without vision, we perish; we become "wild and confused." Unconsciously we agree with the prospect of death ruling over us, which, like that Roman imperial order, drapes itself with other words as a matter of course. Successful subjugation was called "pacification" by the Romans; their system of economically plundering poor people with the help of the military apparatus had the beautiful name *pax romana*. We call war "defense," state terror "order," the goal of world rule "security," and extorted consent "democracy." The subjugated people without vision—whom the Bible calls so realistically "wild and depraved" (Prov. 29:18, Luther's translation), in other words, outwardly aggressive and inwardly empty—are passed off as orderly, peaceful, and "normal."

A little historical review could remind us of a vision that for a short time was not the cause of conscious minorities and the few, but the universal property of a stricken people who understood the greatest disaster of their history as arising at enormous cost through their own fault. I remember the years between 1944 and 1947, a time which had as its climax the capitulation of 8 May 1945. At that time there was a kind of vision in Germany—East and West. Millions of people believed in the depths of their hearts: Never again! No more war! Still a man like Franz Josef Strauss declared that even if his right arm fell off he would not reach for a rifle once more. There was a broad consensus among people when they said, "Never again!" This was a vision that certainly was not clear enough and was largely defined only negatively, since the origins were not reflected. Only a conscious minority addressed the causes of the disaster and added "No more Fascism!" to "No more war!"

Nevertheless, there was a community of the zero hour, which all too soon disappeared. The Adenauer regime and Germany's rearmament can be described as the loss of this vision. The birthright of this vision, originating in shame and horror, was exchanged for the pottage of the economic miracle. West Germany was pampered with the Marshall plan and in a short time developed magnificently and powerfully in its economy. The price of this miracle was integration into the Western military alliance and the remilitarization of West and then East Germany. The vision of a neutral land fell into oblivion except for minorities. When the commanding Western power began a new escalation of the madness in the early eighties to recover its first-strike capability and military superiority, some of the old questions resurfaced in a new way. With the new fear that our country was planned as the battlefield of an integrated warfare uniting nuclear and chemical weapons in its "forward defense," more and more people in Germany remembered the old vision of "Never again!" Slowly this vision is taking more concrete form: a peaceful demilitarized Germany in the heart of Europe, which does not constantly aim at aggressive economic growth and shares less and less the exploitation of the third world. There are good historical reasons that the ecopacifist orientation could gain a foothold in Germany but not with our neighbors beyond the Rhine. For us, in contrast to France, the vision of "Never again!" is bound with guilt and shame. A supportive vision that one day can have a majority on its side must have roots in history and enter into the memory of people.

Beyond the historically mediated vision we need another vision of a peace based on justice, not military force, going back to the beginnings of the human race. Our visions need nourishment. Living in a time of hunger we cannot afford to forget the most ancient visions of humanity.

People

> O land of love! I am yours,
> often angry and crying that you,
> always the idiot, deny your own soul.
> (Hölderlin, "Song of the Germans")

The Bible speaks directly about the "people" that perish without vision. This self-testimony is thoroughly lost to us Germans in this century. After the German catastrophe, not only nationalism seemed ended with all its racist patriarchal undertones, its pointless self-adulation, its arrogance and ignorance, but also every form of national feeling, of the consciousness of being a part of a whole that we call nation. Questions of national identity seem entirely antiquated and incidental for young people traveling through western Europe by rail and for their culture, which in nearly all areas from cuisine to music is more international than national. Consumerism, as Giovanni Pablo Pasolini described it, seems to have done away with every form of national identity, even in Italy, for example.

This changed in the early eighties. West Germans suddenly saw that they live in an "occupied country," a fact that for a long time was not even noticed. When the governing state authorities had to look on helplessly as recreational areas were made the training grounds, when the official of a district could not find out what was actually stored in the native earth in chemical weapons, when the noise of practicing military aircraft made the little children cry, long repressed questions of national sovereignty awakened again.

Through 110,000 low-level flights of the military, infants and older citizens have been injured in their health. Are we an occupied land? Are we just as dependent as the other Germany on our superpower—despite our often invoked freedom? With the new escalation of madness, the questions also intensify about what "the people" really means.

Traditionally, the critical minority of the left has not had an adequate answer to this question. Nation, native country, and home were embarrassing words that one preferred to avoid, especially in postwar Germany. In the United States there is an interesting self-critical discussion today in which people from the large peace and civil rights movements ask why the political left is so weak and powerless within America with its democratic possibilities. Has protest not arisen regarding many individual themes such as racism, militarism, and ecological questions and also been taken up by critical movements? I recall the 1982 peace demonstration in Central Park in New York with over a million people demanding an exodus from the merry-go-round of insanity.

One answer to this question about the weakness of the left is the thesis that essential values and basic attitudes were not articulated but denied and concealed in Marxist and neo-Marxist social analysis. Three central values were profoundly neglected: the family, the nation, and religion. Family, flag, and religion were abandoned to the right wing and defined by them—as though these themes were unworthy from the beginning of a critical analysis, as though the feelings connected with them were irrational and dangerous, as though an enlightened *man* [*sic*] had nothing to do with these realities! Orthodox Marxism did not know how to contribute to these themes, and the critical liberal attitude of many intellectuals was also uninterested in the values that represented a stable, unquestionable foundation for the politics and living standards of the conservative side.

The time has come for this blindness on the part of the left to disappear. It is not enough to unmask religion as the opium of the people, to bid farewell to the family as a coercive patriarchal institution, and to abandon national consciousness as jingoism or (even worse) well-deserved ridiculousness. The critical-liberationist position toward these questions cannot be the abolition of the existential contexts, as ultraleftists often think, but their transformation. The response to these spheres of life—religion, family, and nation—cannot be an unproductive, disclaiming, superhuman "No" but a critical, transforming "Yes, but not this kind of religion, family, and patriotism," full of love of reality.

Religion? Yes, but not this religion that lies and defers. We must finally learn to ask: What are the liberating moments and what are the oppressive moments within a historically given religious tradition? Family? Yes; several generations living together is an elementary human necessity. We need other, liberating forms that overcome patriarchy, but not the simple prevention of the problem in favor of the existence of single people! What is the meaning of nation, people, and native country for our communal existence? Did the idea of das Volk, "the people," definitively die with Hitler?

There are two essentially different orientations in speaking about national identity. There is a national consciousness from above and one from below. In our language people is used in two very different ways, geopolitically and sociopolitically. Geopolitically, what is central is the community of inhabitants of a specific area, a living space where people are joined by history, a common language, and culture. Sociopolitically, what is crucial is a simple, common, lowly people— not in opposition to other countries but in opposition to the powerful. In one case, the delimitation is social within the geopolitical area; in the other case, it happens only outwardly. Holding both meanings together and not isolating them from one another is vital. For the people, speaking geopolitically I emphasize the longings for justice and peace. These desires naturally unite the people with other races and peoples. There is a "patriotism of the poor," as Eduardo Galeano once said, just as there is a religion of the poor that has to be distinguished from the patriotism and religion of the rich.

Personally, I first came to a greater national consciousness through long sojourns abroad. For me it could only develop in the central experiences of German history in this century amid shame and guilt as the natural feelings of a German of my generation. For example, living in the United States I sensed that people who heard me at a public lecture observed me first and above all as a German, that is, not as a woman, Christian, and pacifist but as a member of the nation that murdered their relatives. Gradually I noticed that I could not build any trust without an inner clarity over my identity as a German, originating in the age of poisonous gas. Again and again I felt it necessary to begin sentences with: "I would say as a German. . . ." I regarded concealing my experiences as a game of hide-and-seek and a lie. There is no way around collective responsibility, not even for the younger ones. I am responsible for the house I did not build but inhabit. We live in a historical context; we use the same language that the Nazis used. When I use an innocent word like *Stern*, "star," in a poem, I have to know what I am doing and what others have done with this word in my mother tongue. I think many people find out that it is in a foreign land that one first becomes a German; that is, one learns shame for one's own people and learns to be proud of one's own people. Without these two elementary feelings, shame and pride, national consciousness is empty, hollow, and therefore dangerous.

What distinguishes our situation, in living after the greatest historical catastrophe of our people, from the situation of the French, for example, is that with a certain sensitivity, we act so easily with shame and rage but find it difficult to act with pride. I have often wondered why my parents gave birth to me in this land of night and fog, of officers' clubs and their jokes! Would I not have been much better off if I were Dutch or Portuguese? These are abstract daydreams that avoid reality. Like my sex as a woman and my height, my country is not a matter of my choosing. Becoming adult means integrating these portions of fate in my life, accepting myself as a woman, as small, and also as a German. How much I'd like to say "O land of love!" However, Neuengamme is near Hamburg, and Buchenwald is near Weimar. I still see only how my land, "always the idiot" with weak eyes, denies its own soul.

My shame and my love grew together and produced my patriotism. My love for those who speak my language, who dwell in similar houses, whose dead are buried in German cemeteries, and who make a special potato salad makes me angry about the dreadful destruction and self-annihilation done by my people living without vision. Why do I want the vision of peace and justice, which is still borne by a minority, to be the vision of the majority? If I cut myself off from my people, that cannot be a matter of indifference to me. I could emigrate before reunification in the common grave takes place. If I did not love my land, I would not need to be so frightfully ashamed.

Another dimension of "the people" that is extremely threatened today is involved in this consciousness of national cohesion that I appropriated so late. If I judge the economic policies of the eighties correctly, I see them as a denunciation of the most elementary responsibilities for one another, as an earlier order called the "national" economy represented them. It is a governmentally directed denunciation of the solidarity agreements between young and old, sick and healthy, workers and the unemployed. Today the government seems to me intent on abolishing the *bonum commune*, the common well-being of all people in the community, which exists for all and to which all have a right, without regard to performance. Disintegration into individual interest groups has advanced so far that among leaders consciousness of bearing responsibility has become obsolete. The state, whose legitimation can rest only on its responsibility for the whole, in particular for its weakest parts, has removed itself so far from basic ideas of responsibility for the health, employment, and peace of its citizens that we can speak of the dismissal of the *bonum commune*.

I do not like to use the word *state*. I know that many members of the young generation associate this word with police cudgels and tear gas, not with my old European *bonum commune*. By a just state I imagine a community where the interests and needs of the weakest are protected and emphasized. In one example, information policy after Chernobyl, I would like to make clear the possible meaning of true state responsibility today. A few days after the reactor catastrophe, the great popular festival, "Rhine Ablaze," was to be celebrated by about 300,000 people. Heavy rains were anticipated that night, and with this rain the radioactive fall-out would fall on people. The ambulance operators of the lifesaving organizations on duty had orders to go into tents when the radioactive rain came. Whoever got wet from the rain was to take a shower in any case. No one warned the 300,000 people. They were wet up to their necks. The state had acquitted itself of its responsibility. It was a crime not to warn people. The festival should have been canceled.

In the prophet Isaiah there is a vision of peace after national catastrophe. The time of disaster and the time of blessing are represented in images of nature, the land, harvest, and fruit. The dreadful experience that "the wilderness grows," as Nietzsche said later and as the catastrophe of Chernobyl confirmed almost literally, is juxtaposed with the vision that the wilderness will again become a garden.

> In little more than a year
>   you will shudder . . .
> for the vintage will fail,
>   the fruit harvest will not come.
> Tremble, you women who are at ease,
>   shudder, you complacent ones.
>
>   .   .   .   .
>
> Beat your breasts for the pleasant fields,
>   for the fruitful vine,
> for the soil of my people
>   growing up in thorns and briers;
> yes, for all the joyous houses
>   in the jubilant city.
> For the palace will be forsaken,
>   the populous city deserted;
> the hill and the watchtower
>   will become dens forever,
> the joy of wild asses,
>   a pasture for flocks;

until a spirit from on high is poured out on us,
  and the wilderness becomes a fruitful field.

. . . .

The effect of righteousness will be peace,
  and the result of righteousness, quietness and trust forever.
My people will abide in a peaceful habitation,
  in secure dwellings, and in quiet resting places.

(Isa. 32:10–18, abridged)

Remembrance and Hope

The remembrance of real history could be dangerous to the remembrance concocted out of self-protection and hatred of foreigners. It could disturb the submissiveness of those who remember. In this hope I am not thinking so much of the phenomenon of the extreme right wing, the neofascism of those who hold Auschwitz to be a lie, and so forth. The politically dangerous function of these marginal groups is not their cemetery desecration and other abominations but their determining the climate even for the nonextreme middle-class majority that defines itself as "center." With the politics of *perestroika* and *glasnost*, their mentality has shifted further to the right. The Nazis were abominable, but we do not need to talk about that anymore today (excuse); the Russians are even worse, as seen in Nicaragua (denial of reality); if neutralization is our ultimate end, we must rearm (destructive will).

A people without vision cannot remember. Several years ago I, along with others, heard an elderly concentration camp survivor relate his experiences. For over twenty years I had not heard anyone who was a member of the communist party speak about this past. But here, in a church, it was possible to listen to an older communist. This in itself was remarkable, since there is generally hardly any publicity for the marginalized in Germany and its media. The church, it occurred to me, is an arena of freedom not only for former East Germany but for all of Germany.

One story we heard affected me very much. Radio
Moscow broadcast lists of German war prisoners. German
communists listened to these broadcasts, wrote down the
names, found out the addresses, and notified the relatives.
This little event gives substance to the idea of "remembrance" in the national sense. I would not like this story to
be forgotten. I do not want those who risked their lives at
that time to disappear from the history of German resistance against the Nazis. I compared the evening with the
aged communist with my daily experiences with anticom-
munism and wrote a poem contrasting a loud voice in my
country with a soft voice.

Concentration Camp Number
Eight Thousand Four Hundred Twenty-Four

How could you cooperate with them
I am asked

> radio moscow to which we were forbidden to listen
> by the death penalty
> published in 1943 lists of German prisoners

if you are part of them, all is lost
I am warned

> these people wrote down all the names
> therefore they're also subject to the death penalty

you make yourself unbelievable
they threaten me

> then they sent anonymous letters to the relatives
> with only two words printed: HE LIVES

> This message I know from old times
> it is the Easter message
> whose multiplication at that time
> was subject to the death penalty

God is memory, according to process theologians. Without memory, without knowledge of what was, we are free of God. Those who do not remember are forced to reexperience what is repressed. This insight of psychoanalysis has an extraordinary significance for reflective persons in Germany, apart from the rest of western Europe. The deepest motivation of people in turning against forced rearmament is found in their historical experience. People, even younger persons, reconnect with the experiences of forty years ago. "No more war!" suddenly reappeared at the beginning of the eighties. A national consciousness spanning the generations is present. We in this land in the heart of Europe have a special responsibility to say no to war preparation, which is only veiled by the word *armament*.

"No more war!" is connected with a productive feeling of guilt and shame. "This time no one can say he did not know" is one of the guiding principles inscribed in recent years on the walls of houses and in pamphlets. This is a very German sentence that I can scarcely imagine in other countries. It is one of the basic experiences of my generation. I was fifteen when the war ended and then spent ten years of my adult life asking: What did you do then, Mr. Teacher, Mr. Professor; where were you then, dear father, dear mother; what did you accomplish during that time? This was the basic question of my generation. An author like Günter Grass raised this question in *The Tin Drum* to invent a person who refused to grow up and remained a dwarf: Oscar the drummer. This is a clear example of what my generation felt. How can one grow up in such a world? How can one want to be an adult with such German parents?

The worst answer to the question, Where were you? was always the same: "We did not know. Unfortunately we had no Jewish acquaintances. It was not so bad for us in the village. Yes, we once heard of a concentration camp, but only communists and criminals were there." This language, this elemental lie of the adult generation, perplexed me tremendously. Nevertheless, this is a part of the work of the peace movement that people are not able to express anymore. Today no one can say any longer that he or she did not know who produced the new weapons, what capacities they have, why they are stationed among us, what a first-strike strategy is, what a deep strike is, and so forth. No one can claim that he or she did not know that our land was being made into the battlefield of a "limited" nuclear war! One of the historical merits of the peace movement is its stress on what is at stake.

The historical consciousness of the reflective minority insisting on its position cannot be denied by the majority of others taking positions friendly to the military—whether out of indifference or out of conviction. All people have witnessed that war follows armament. Everyone has at least heard the question, "What did you do when they picked up your neighbors?" even if they did not ask it themselves. There is an accumulated moral knowledge of the past called *conscience* in our language, which can form a mountain range out of a mountain. In this sense there is a minority of conscience today. This cognitive minority does not gain its strength from a simple accusatory identification—as if all Germans were Nazis! This is not true and never was. However, all Germans knew or could have known what was at stake. Therefore the current majority, which still clings to Western propaganda, cannot silence the minority.

The minority of conscience remembers and seeks to remind others. It has ceased repressing or trivializing national guilt and collective shame; it does not babble about its "grace of late birth" (an expression Chancellor Kohl coined). The minority of conscience accepts the dreadful inheritance and makes it productive as protest, refusal, and resistance. Out of the suffering history of shame and guilt, this minority is developing another vision of a liberated Europe in which forging swords into plowshares will be allowed.

The intellectual process of this conversion of national shame into the desire for peace, of humble remembrance into power, of knowledge into readiness for struggle, is an essential historical experience of the eighties. In the language of religion I would call this new transforming power a "revival." Out of the sleep of dependence, people rise up for peace. Old terms—like *sovereignty of the people, home, self-determination, occupied* or *liberated area*—come to mind again. The old forms of religious expression surface—such as entrance processions, setting up penitential crosses, prayer liturgies. Worship services are celebrated near barbed wire protecting the new death plants within our land, in Mutlangen, Wackersdorf, Hunsrück, and many other places, The experiences of history become the brilliant weapon displays of beautiful tactical aircraft and nuclear plants juxtaposed with photos of Dresden and Hiroshima. This new historical awareness ready for action condenses into simple, clear, and incontestable sentences. "War follows rearmament."

Fifty years ago Kurt Tucholsky wrote: "People have never seriously attempted combating war. All the schools and all the churches, all the movie houses and all the newspapers have never been barred from the propaganda of war. One does not even know what a generation would look like that grew up in the air of a healthy pacifism, joyful in struggle but rejecting war. How can one know this? We only know politically fanaticized youth." These words are only partly true today. Alongside the "politically fanaticized" youth, there is youth with a different relationship to truth. The necessary questions are being raised.

There are whole school classes that stand confused and speechless today before the photos and documents of Bergen-Belsen. "How could that happen?" they ask. At times I think something similar will be possible at the end of the century with whole school classes facing photos of the misery and starvation in India or Africa and asking: How could that happen? In other words, how could we have endured all that and constantly rearmed? How could the people have actually allowed that?

Yes, how? How do we deal with the terror reports striking us daily? How do we react when we hear the medical recommendation to breast-feed children no more than four months on account of the heavy metals in mother's milk? How do we live in the here and now with the prospect of death ruling us? What place in our thoughts and emotions do we grant to the question of justice, which is the question about God's future? Naming the misery and having full knowledge of catastrophes is not enough. A knowledge that is not concretized in our conduct only contributes to our paralysis. The intellectual situation of the enlightened middle class in the first world—presumably including many readers—can be paraphrased by saying we are overeducated and underpowered. To us knowledge does not mean power, as in the working-class movement of the nineteenth century, but deeper and more bitter powerlessness. Being conscious of our situation, nationally and internationally, has for us a moment of desperate drug dependence: we surpass one another in knowledge of catastrophe. Knowledge is indeed more necessary than ever, since one cannot hear, see, taste, or smell radioactive rays, but our knowledge smacks only of death. This situation of powerlessness, of everyday helplessness toward low-flying aircraft, radioactively contaminated mushrooms, and fruit from South Africa poisoned by apartheid, is unbearable and forces us to repress. We prefer denying knowledge and pretending to be dead to enduring our own impotence. Even those who bear political responsibility and wield power feel their lack of sovereignty in elementary questions of "security" policy and flee into repression of reality.

In Aachen in May 1985 four youths committed collective suicide. One seventeen-year-old wrote in a farewell letter:

> Life here on earth is simply insane, only a waste of time. . . . People build bombs even though they have so many. People think only of destroying. Do they think at all about the animals or trees? No. Or the rivers and our air? I will be in paradise. . . . Mama and papa, you were the best parents in the world. Don't be sad, okay? We will see each other again.
>
> Your Bohne
>
> P.S. Jorg Heinrich, you get my cassettes and my black cap. Farewell.

Wavering here and there between repression of reality and powerlessness, we need such visions of God's future.

Our helplessness and repression intensify one another. Because we believe ourselves impotent, we have to pretend that we see nothing. Since we concentrate our efforts on this repression, we have no energy anymore to overcome our powerlessness and to act according to the biblical vision. The freest people in our country, in fact, are those who act in resistance against the idols of technological progress and military omnipotence without having to repress. In this context the Bible has become increasingly important for many groups. The Bible has not come closer to us, but we have come closer to the Bible, since our real situation as a minority living in a violent empire has great similarity with the situation of the New Testament. The conduct of the first Christians in this empire of exploitation and permanent war preparation becomes more and more clear to us. When Paul says that we are either slaves of sin or slaves of Christ, I am confronted with a picture that contradicts my liberal consciousness. Today I have a much deeper understanding of slavery to sin and upholding its rule through taxes, consumption, and cooperation. Setting out with Christ on another way has also become clearer to me.

A conversion from certain values now styled "fundamental" is part of a vision of the "land where it will be easier to be good." Justice is nearer the fountain of life than security; renouncing power opens up more freedom than the use of power. Recognizing mutual dependence is necessary to live in the "global village" we inhabit. This mutuality and dependence also respect our fellow creatures who do not speak our language. Peace with nature, not against nature, is a way of respecting the creation that we have unlearned in Western industrial history. Can we learn it again?

The Bible says that our "young people shall see visions" (Joel 2:28 [Heb. 3:1]; Acts 2:17). Visions are vital, and the remembrance of the vision of the end is a feast that joins us together and is to be celebrated again and again. In church language this celebration is called "divine service" or worship, and an inalienable element of such assemblies of people in God's name is the vision of our sharing and being nourished from the religious tradition. From this shared vision grows a strength for resistance. A worship service without vision is empty; vision illuminates and warms. Some readers of this book may react with uneasiness and cynicism to the attempted remembrance of God's future. "O how beautiful that would be" is an expression of this mild or sarcastic cynicism. We have already renounced so much in our hopes and so mutilated our understanding of justice that we often no longer even dare to lift our eyes to the hills from whence comes our help (Ps. 121:1). Nevertheless, this lifting of our eyes, this everyday perseverance, this incorporating our own vision into conscience and sharing it with our tradition and the tradition of the people beside us—this is a process as natural as breathing. Without it we revert to a suicide that the Bible often calls "death." How can we answer those who sadly shrug their shoulders and bury their liveliness along with their wishes?

Hope and illusion have to be distinguished. This distinction cannot be understood from the outside. Intelligent observers who do not share the vision of God's people will consider it naive and overly optimistic. Spellbound by the question of power, they know how to prove the powerlessness of the social movements for peace, solidarity with the peoples of the third world, and reconciliation with nature. That the gentle water will break the stone is incredible to them. They see from the outside whether life ends well or badly. However, this standpoint of the observer is not really possible when one's life is at stake. A hope that waits for results and does not really identify with what is expected is only the sandbox of inner intuitions and in this sense is mere illusion.

Christian hope in the tradition of the supernatural virtues, that is, of virtues poured into us by grace, is distinguished from the hope of the observer by sharing, cooperation, and participation. Christian hope is hope in which I share in the production of another state. The hope of peace lives with the peacemakers and not beyond them. Participation in the struggle distinguishes this hope from the contemplative observation that is optimistic one moment and resigned the next. At the beginning of the eighties in a school in Boston, there was an opinion poll about the probability of a nuclear war. All the children except one thought that the end of the world was near. When asked why he did not believe in nuclear war, the child with the differing opinion proclaimed: "'Cause Mom and Dad are working against it."

Only within the resistance movement is there hope. Struggle is our teacher, said Che Guevara. Let me add: hope. Only when one offers oneself in this struggle can hope come out of expectation. As long as we are still in the spectator position, counting how many missiles are on both sides, how many people have demonstrated, how many congresspeople are on the side of disarmament, and so forth, we still have not identified with the hope for which we are prepared to risk our own life, our own vitality, energy, time, and money.

When hope becomes existential in this sense, hope brings forth two loving daughters, namely, anger and courage. As the church father Augustine said, there is anger that the nothingness remains nothing, and courage that what should be will be. In the words of a native North American who is a medicine man:

> If [being] militant means
> that I use every possibility
> that I take every possible step and
> every possible action
> to introduce
> once and for all
> the natural way of life of humanity,
> then I ask my father sun
> and my mother earth
> to give me life and strength
> to be
> the most militant of all.

CHAPTER FIVE

On Earth as in the West

Since the East is now in the West, the enemy, as everybody knows, is in the South. George Bush has said very clearly what this means in his address on the state of the union. Now a new historical epoch begins, even a new world order. What is new is that it is supported by the unity of world opinion. That the United States stands in first place in this world order is not very new, but it is still important for the president to declare it. This world order began with a war, a new kind of war in which psychological warfare has been decisively improved. This war is only the first of many North-South wars that can be expected. On a journey through Latin America I heard only one question from many people following the Gulf war: "Which country will be next after Panama and Iraq?" On earth as in the West. . . .

Nowadays I miss the clear voice of my late friend Erich Fried. He had enlightened the confusion in which many find themselves. I see a new "declaration of bankruptcy by intellectuals" and recall the justification of war in the intellectual disaster of 1914. We must quickly shift gears: from the war motive of correcting Saddam Hussein's injustice to the motive of preventive war for Israel. In this framework the welcome opportunity was provided for defaming the German peace movement. Ernst Tugendhat wrote: "There are people and even states who can play on the irrational guilt feelings of another as masterfully as on a piano." This playing continues. The absurd situation has arisen that some try to dismiss the peace movement—which has labored on the real guilt feelings of the nation as hardly any other—with the suspicion of anti-Semitism. I would like to recall just one sentence from this movement, one that can only be understood with the memory of Auschwitz, that marvelous and thoroughly German sentence: "This time no one can say that he did not know." Nevertheless, in the West the focus is not on reflection on the past but rather on preventive wars, not on disarmament but rearmament, not on caring, with drinking water for those reduced to misery, but new epidemics, of which cholera is only the most visible. The money consumed in one day of the Gulf war would be enough for the little country of Peru to have cleaner water for everyone.

"On Earth as in Heaven" was the title of the Berlin People's University celebration on Pentecost (1991). This title is theologically excellent. Theology is the distinction between God and the idols, between the God of life and the idols of oppression. The title points us to this task. "Thy will be done on earth, as it is in heaven," we say in the Lord's Prayer. That the will of God is discernible is assumed. "You shall not kill" is another sentence of the same God.

Among us the West pretends to be a kind of heaven: new world order, uniform opinion, new armament thrusts, total rule over all other peoples. The idol that is worshiped there is sheer power. In contrast to this Christians pray for the realization of God's will and refer to the universalist traditions of life for all humanity. It is not at all simple not to mistake the West for heaven, since it is constantly drummed into us.* It also is not simple to ally ourselves with the God of life and continue resisting. Since the East now lies in the West, we will have to learn this again in the West as in the East.

---

* There is a neat, but untranslatable, double pun in the author's German sentence. *Himmel* means both "sky" and "heaven," and in the second clause *eingebläut*, "blued in," brings to mind its homophone *eingebleut*, "drummed in."—ED.

CHAPTER SIX

Moses, Jesus, and Marx:
Utopians in Search of Justice

"Do you still believe in that, little child?" an elderly Jewish woman friend in the United States asked me. "Look: Moses on Sinai, Jesus of Nazareth, and Karl Marx from Trier. There are three Jewish attempts to humanize humanity. . . . Rather futile, it seems to me." This sarcasm came to my mind again when I read the sentence on a building wall in the former East Germany: "Marx is dead and Jesus lives!" My elderly friend had combined the three Jews from world history because they all formulated the conditions for a more just society at definite historical turning points: Moses, in the transition from nomadic to agricultural society, designated human rights in the form of the Ten Commandments; Jesus of Nazareth, living under the despotism and militarism of the Roman Empire, proclaimed a nonviolent ethic, the Sermon on the Mount; and Karl Marx, under industrial capitalism, gave the old hopes of people a new form in scientific socialism. Are all three dead? Moses, who deciphered "You shall not murder" as the message of the mysterious God? Jesus, with his absurd idea not to prepare to kill or bomb away one's enemies but to love them? And Karl Marx, who wanted to overturn "all conditions in which people are degraded, abandoned, or held in contempt"? Are not all three dead because they are absolutely useless for the Gulf war and the rearmament of NATO, for the International Monetary Fund and the permanent war against the poorest? Did these Jewish attempts to live differently in a shalom of peace and justice not ultimately fail?

"Marx is dead and Jesus lives." Was Karl Marx dead because Jesus lives and has conquered? Unfortunately I do not see much of that. I would like to raise three simple questions: Who won? Who lost? Where is God?

Who Won?

The first question—Who actually won?—was very clear to me when a Christian journal in the United States asked me in an interview: "Some read present events in eastern Europe and the Soviet Union as a triumph of democracy in the best sense. Others see it as a triumph of capitalism and individualism in the worst sense. How do you understand this turnabout?" With this either-or I could do nothing. I had to condescend to take up an idea that I had avoided for a long time, the idea of "democratic capitalism," about which Christian thinkers in the States speak in beautiful openness. This idea seems clearer to me than the idea of the "social market economy," preferred among us, where I never know exactly how far the adjective social really extends with rents, land prices, unemployment, medical care, and many other questions. I think these two elements, democracy and capitalism, have won against the bureaucratically centralized coercive organization. The people have actually chosen bananas and freedom of the press, Italian vacations and respect for human rights, free enterprise and unemployment. The state-socialist attempting at building a solidarity society has failed—and not only in Europe.

The reasons for this failure can be identified in many places: a concentration of political power without opposition, a bureaucracy that left people without rights and apathetic, the command economy without individual incentives, corruption without any democratic controls by the media, extreme militarism, which even today—in Russia—still commissions and serves itself. The abolition of private property in the means of production in no way removed the naturally growing interests and inequalities but multiplied them in other forms of the domination of people over people. State-socialist education led to qualities like adaptation, cringing before bosses, and cynicism toward one's own critical convictions. A determinism from the philosophy of history, which asserted the destruction of capitalism and the victory of socialism as scientific predictions, was not disturbed by any sense of reality; it contributed decisively to the dogmatization of specific intellectual positions. A falsely understood materialism did not see human corporeality and our membership in nature. Instead, nature was regarded as an object of subjugation under human rule. The fact that we human beings *are* nature and do not play only the role of exploiter in relation to the natural foundations of life was overlooked in the eastern and western intellectual systems of industrialism.

Who Lost?

The victory of democratic capitalism over state socialism does not represent only liberation of people from indebted and inflicted dependence. This victory has its price today and will demand even more terrible sacrifice in the future. I think once again of the weakest members of the state-socialist society, who had the insufficient but real protection of their lodgings, their health insurance, and their jobs in the previous order. I think of the many unqualified older persons, useless in our system, who were dragged from the factories. A psychiatrist told me of her recuperating patients, whom she can no longer send to the factories because the factories now have only one single function, namely, making a profit. Many of the weaker people who had found a niche, a hiding place in which to survive in the unproductive system, have lost. The women who can no longer sue for a place in the kindergarten and who are the first dismissed, because they are sometimes absent on account of their children, have lost. The older women with their little pensions also lost when transportation and postage rates multiplied. The feminization of poverty is already planned.

The Victory of Democratic Capitalism Has Its Price

In a global context very different groups and peoples have lost something. I think of the two-thirds, soon three-fourths, of the world population who are poor. For a long time Marxist theory has turned its attention away from the industrial proletariat as a bearer of hope to the impoverished masses of the third world. The turn from Marxism to neo-Marxism, which included world trade relations with the third world, was a fundamental change in Marxist theory. The collapse of state socialism meant the death of one hope of people deprived of their rights. Perhaps I should say: the right to dream of another way of life was taken from them. Capitalism no longer needs to fear that subjugated peoples could prefer another model. They have no choice anymore. That Cuba will fail in its present form is only a question of time. One may argue whether the liberation movements of the third-world nations sought eastern state socialism. Certainly it was not the Moscow system of informers and work standards, bureaucracy and militarism that attracted them. Many of them have emphasized again and again that their own way to freedom had to be a third way. In this regard Nicaragua, with its experiment of a mixed economy and a multiparty system, has certainly been a model for many other countries. However, the superpower could not tolerate this deviation from the true way of free enterprise.

Hunger, Misery, and Growing Debt

That the capitalist way brings hunger, misery, and increasing indebtedness for the peoples of the third world has been evident for a long time and, since the debt crisis, can no longer be denied even by the most obstinate defenders of democratic capitalist development. In the last seven years the poor countries have transferred more money to the rich lands than they have received in developmental aid. The question resulting from the analysis of the third world is whether there is any

kind of hope anymore for the poor under the absolute
monarchy of capitalism. Must they play the role of raw material suppliers and cheap work slaves forever? Must they give
away their lands for military bases and toxic waste dumps,
and their children to prostitution?

The democratic element that makes capitalism tolerable,
profitable, and—within limits—legally secure at the center
fails along the periphery. The most barbaric military dictator-
ships were supported for decades by the superpowers when
they only guaranteed privileges, power, markets, and tax advantages for capital. None of this has been changed by the
fetish of free elections. It is part of the nature of democratic
capitalism that on the plane of world trade relations, it needs
democratic masks not at all or only as an occasional disguise.

Conditions Worse Than in Early Capitalism

The socialist movement in Europe has gained a great deal
from capitalism in a struggle lasting over a hundred years:
the abolition of child labor, wage continuation in case of
sickness, the reduction of working hours from the fourteen-
hour day to the forty-hour week. union organization and the
protection it gives, the right to strike, and minor forms of
codetermination. But all these benefits of a capitalism tamed
in its brutality, which we have taken for granted for so long,
are lacking in the third world. Conditions there are worse
than in the Manchester or Wuppertal of early capitalism.
The problems of economic systems built on the greed of in-
dividuals for profit have shifted today into the third world.
European socialism did not fail in democratizing and hu-
manizing capitalism. It failed in the attempt to replace capitalism. It played a historical role in the humanization of the
industrial system, but this role of democratic socialism was
limited. It has decisively improved working conditions in industrial countries but did not attack imperialism and its
misanthropic shadow, militarism. Whoever speaks today
about the social market economy without mentioning the
death market and the weapons economy veils reality.

Exploiting Creation

Capitalism has won its battle with state socialism and turned out to be more stable and life-enhancing. But the poor—a third here in the West and three-quarters of the whole human family—have lost. Still there will be another victim of free enterprise: our mother, the earth. Will the mechanisms of the market be able to prevent ecological catastrophe? The North's model of civilization cannot be generalized; it is not even true for the North. A world with three billion autos, four hundred million tons of meat, forty million megawatts of electrical capacity, and twelve billion tons of oil per year is not possible on this planet. Thus the promise of capitalism that everyone can share in the wealth and prosperity cannot be redeemed socially and is also ecologically totally hopeless, without a future. Does capitalism not have the same relation to nature as state socialism? It treats nature like women, like savages, like objects that have to be investigated and penetrated so they can be controlled and exploited. Capitalism does not have any notion of beauty other than commercialization.

Capitalism can be criticized not only because of the exploitation that it inflicts on the majority but also on account of its destruction of human desires. I quote from the Sermon on the Mount: "Do not lay up for yourselves treasures on earth, where moth and rust consume and where thieves break in and steal; but store up for yourselves treasures in heaven, where neither moth nor rust consumes and where thieves do not break in and steal. For where your treasure is, there your heart will be also" (Matt. 6:19–21). The ability to desire, to dream, and to yearn is part of human nature. We do not know another person when we do not know her or his vision. We know too little about ourselves when we do not know the treasure of which Jesus speaks. I recall that as a hungry postwar child I dreamed of spaghetti. My desires were reduced to a single point. The oppressed in the Roman Empire call their vision in the Bible a "new heaven and a new earth." Between this little, reduced desire and the great utopias we live, and the bird that we are flies. A central project of capitalism is to clip the wings of the bird so that the bird reinterprets its desires. The person must first be made *homo oeconomicus* and the money fetish made boundless and omnipotent. A young man said, when asked about his future: "If I am not a millionaire by 30, I will kill myself." So the bird has been made perfectly happy.

Is Marx really dead? What role will socialism play in overcoming capitalism? That capitalism must change, since all people cannot play havoc with energy like the rich in industrial countries, can hardly be contested anymore today. The question is rather: When will capitalism recognize at last the limits of growth? Then socialist conceptions will dissolve today's ideologizing of the free market. Let me give a simple example of this problem. In Los Angeles there is a considerable water shortage because of a lack of rain. First there was an attempt to deal with the problem in a capitalist way. The price of drinking water was greatly increased. This strategy did not produce any changes in behavior: the rich filled their swimming pools, and the poor were encumbered with debts or stopped washing. Riots threatened. In a second effort the city tried methods of planned conservation: a definite amount of water was apportioned to every household, and overuse was controlled and severely punished. This time they succeeded in stabilizing the situation.

The supposed death of socialism means that capitalism confirms itself as the only possible basis for human existence. Once and for all time capitalism is absolutely necessary and also has the will, ideologically speaking, to destroy hope and solidarity in the social spirituality of every human being. Where your treasure is, namely, in the bank, there your heart will be also. In other words, the life-world (Jürgen Habermas, *The Crisis of Legitimacy*) is dominated and colonized in total capitalism.

The earth has become a colony of capitalism. In all preindustrial societies the individual was not defined exclusively as *homo oeconomicus*. He and she were beings who also engaged in singing, praying, and playing, creating myths and giving meaning, things now regarded as superfluous, not purposefully rational. Economic instrumental reason clips the wings of the bird so it can no longer fly. People fall into the traps of working and consuming and ignore the limitations of nature and the limitations of material needs. In a kind of production mania—without limits, without a sabbath, and without a consciousness of death—the material world-culture that appears without alternative is accepted as the only possible culture. Habermas speaks of the "pointless violence of our culture. Today the world market and television alone, if they do not come to the barbarism of highly technological warfare, provide in anonymous ways what was once embodied in colonial masters and missionaries" (J. Habermas, *Vergangenheit als Zukunft* [The Past as Future], Pendo Profile [Zurich, 1991], 126). That we submit to this false authority is the spiritual death in which we live. The perfectly happy bird remains of itself in the cage. On television this cage appears unlimited, infinite, and almighty. Why should the bird want to leave it? The religions of most peoples have taught that we must die and that we are capable of God. They spoke emphatically about our limitation and about our boundlessness and dramatized both elemental experiences. They did not start from the reduction of people under economic force.

Where Is God?

State socialism is dead, but socialism as a utopia of solidarity is still urgently needed. The state socialism already de-democratized by Lenin and made into an instrument of terror by Stalin has no chance anymore. However, the poor of the earth have not disappeared, and the problems that need another social order founded on solidarity have not been solved and are not solvable by the enlightened self-interest on which capitalism rests ethically.

When we ask where God is in these two ideologies that have struggled together so long, the answer we hear so often, "with the victors," is plainly wrong. Moses called such answers idolatry, and there is also among us a way of worshiping the golden calf as if it had led the people of East Germany into reunification. But the biblical God is not this phallic bull. The biblical God has taken sides irrevocably with the poor and asks us first how we relate to them. To say, "Marx is dead and Jesus lives," is, in my Christian opinion, an insult to Jesus, who did not come ultimately to bless the capitalist system. Should Jesus rejoice that Marx is dead? We find this kind of competitive thinking today in the right wing of the large churches. No one may presume that the Jesus who came to liberate the poor would hold the worship of wealth to be desirable. "No one can serve two masters. . . . You cannot serve God and wealth." Jesus' interest is that people live together according to the will of God, that they need not prostitute themselves for hunger like the ten to twenty thousand children in Manila. Therefore, within capitalism Jesus asks people today how they relate to the least of their sisters and brothers, and how they realize the will of God that intends life in abundance for all. This question presumably includes a more comprehensive idea of justice than in the horizon of previous socialism, which transcends the moral level of capitalism and demands another economic ethic. To me this seems absolutely necessary.

I am afraid of a purely capitalist world in which the poor become ever poorer and ever more dispensable. Soon we will even be persuaded that it is good when they starve to death as children, since otherwise they would only multiply. The Darwinian cloven hoof of a supposedly rational economic order is visible in such theoretical models of everyday life. I am fearful of restricting the possible, of prohibiting different dreams of the world. Naturally, Jesus and his friends were dreamers and utopians, in other words, people without a place in this world of systematic injustice and misery.

The Utopia of the Man from Nazareth

The poor little man from Nazareth described the utopia with a word from Jewish tradition meaning righteousness or

justice. "Strive first for the kingdom of God and God's righteousness, and all these things will be given to you as well."
There are translations of the Bible in which this word *righteousness* appears more seldom than in others. Can one not
also speak of God's mildness, friendliness, and affability?
Does justice not have this light touch of communism? Is it
not better to avoid the term? After all, Marx is indeed dead!

I do not believe that we can separate Jesus from his Jewish
background and stylize him as a private redeemer of individual souls. Something very different flashes up in Christianity
and acutely disturbs the culture of money and pleasure, violence and careers in which we live. The claim on us as it appears in the New Testament was greater; our yearning
reached further. Even in the midst of the rich world, we have
this longing not to drink coffee and eat bananas at the ex-
pense of others, not to ship our garbage to poor countries, not
to buy and sell objects of sexual lust and get rich by exporting
weapons and poison gas. Planted in us is something of this
utopia of Jesus that we all together may do the will of God,
build a world economic order that is different from this mur-
derous one, and seek a peace that is different from the one
based on A, B, and C (atomic, biological, and chemical)
weapons. Living in us is the desire that the creation of life on
this little blue planet may not be ruined or destroyed. Lodged
in us is "the breath of God," as the Quakers say, the power to
hallow life and not subordinate it to profit. Jesus came to
awaken in us the breath of God that wants to come out, to be
free and visible.

Even in Us There Is Some of This Utopia

The religions have many different names for God that answer the question of where God is to be found. Some stress
silence, the solitariness of the heart, and sinking into the collective unconscious. The biblical tradition has added another
name to the different names of God, and it seldom appears
in the other religions in this strictness and precision. That is
the name righteousness or justice, the heart of our Jewish

and Christian tradition. Without it there can be no prayer, no incense, no meditative absorption. Without the poor there is no nearness to God. Justice is the way that we can discover God. Justice is the will of God. For its sake the Bible speaks incessantly of the poor and warns that the riches we heap up between ourselves and the poor also hide us from God and bar the way to God. Is God then involved in the economic order? The Bible says yes, and it takes sides with the poorest.

No Nearness to God Without the Poor

If we allow the dream that the hungry will be satisfied to be prohibited, then we have separated ourselves from God, or in any case from the God of the Bible. Capitalism does not forbid this dream, because that is not a modern method, but sees to it that we forget the dream. When that does not work, because of troublesome obstructionists like Isaiah and Jesus, another method is introduced: the dream is made ridiculous. Acceptance of utopias is disappearing; the dream of daily bread for all is not on the agenda of the postmodern consciousness. The thousand children who die of hunger every day in Brazil alone have no news value. Perhaps the mild cynicism of our culture is the best deterrent against this ability to believe and imagine, this loving and acting that seeks more in life than we already have. Nevertheless, this deterrent will not function for everyone and certainly not forever. There is something ineradicable about faith, hope, and love. One may criticize the anthropology of previous socialism for being too optimistic. However, the cynical anthropology of real existing capitalism is unbearable for the spiritually gifted. Present reality is not everything! A transcendence stirs within us that cannot be satisfied. Even an economically stable capitalism will not succeed in smothering this stirring. For God wants to believe in us, to hope in us, and to become one with us in love.

PART III
Biblical Roots

PART III

Biblical Topics

CHAPTER SEVEN

God's Second Creation

But God remembered Noah and all the wild animals and all the domestic animals that were with him in the ark. And God made a wind blow over the earth, and the waters subsided; the fountains of the deep and the windows of the heavens were closed, the rain from the heavens was restrained, and the waters gradually receded from the earth. At the end of one hundred and fifty days the waters had abated; and in the seventh month, on the seventeenth day of the month, the ark came to rest on the mountains of Ararat. The waters continued to abate until the tenth month; in the tenth month, on the first day of the month, the tops of the mountains appeared.

At the end of forty days Noah opened the window of the ark that he had made and sent out the raven; and it went to and fro until the waters were dried up from the earth. Then he sent out the dove from him, to see if the waters had subsided from the face of the ground; but the dove found no place to set its foot, and it returned to him to the ark, for the waters were still on the face of the whole earth. So he put out his hand and took it and brought it into the ark with him. He waited another seven days, and again he sent out the dove from the ark; and the dove came back to him in the evening, and there in its beak was a freshly plucked olive leaf; so Noah knew that the waters had subsided from the earth. Then he waited another seven days, and sent out the dove; and it did not return to him any more.

(Gen. 8:1–12)

If there is one text in the Hebrew Bible in which the conventional distinction of the "Old Testament law" and the supposedly non-Jewish "gospel" becomes a disgrace, it is this text. From the first to the last word, it is the pure gospel of the deliverance of creatures through the intent and means of God's will. Here the anti-Jewish distinction is unmasked as

theologically problematical (which cannot be developed here),

historically false, since Judaism is only seen as a distorted caricature,

psychologically intolerably arrogant, and in most cases politically exploited in a reactionary way.

Our pericope *is* liberating news: a great arch spans from God's remembrance (v. 1), which is at the same time God's action (v. 1b), to events in nature (vs. 2–5) in its elements wind and water, to Noah's actions (v. 6), and the collaborating actions of feathered fellow creatures (vs. 7–12). The purpose of this action is the deliverance of beings threatened by death. "God remembered Noah." In this Hebrew word *remember*, thought and action are brought together. All true remembrance has this existential quality of change. "Then God remembered Rachel, and God heeded her and opened her womb" (Gen. 30:22). God's remembering knows no lack of commitment; it establishes communication. We would advance theologically if we replaced God's tranquil eternal omniscience with active temporal "remembering." In his Pentateuch commentary on "God remembered Noah" Rashi (1040–1105) says: "This word stands for the quality of law changed into the quality of mercy by the prayers of the just" (ed. S. Bamberger [Basel, 1975], 21). God and the just, mercy and prayer, belong together in the process of liberation, just as Yahweh's wind and Noah's ability, learned from sailors, to understand the language of birds, are related to each other. Here we have a fragment of great narrative literature like the Gospels themselves. That the story of the rescue is also one involving people and animals (vs. 7–12) reveals the commonality of the deliverance as a plot. As a response to Brecht's well-known saying, "You die with all the animals, and nothing will change," it is a cheerful "You live with all the animals," with an open conclusion.

Floods and Repentance

The earlier story of the great flood has many parallels in the oral narratives of earlier peoples, which were later handed down in a written form in the high cultures of the ancient Orient. Like the creation narratives, the flood narratives are among the cultural achievements of humanity meditating in mythical form upon the origin and endangerment of their world. The great flood, handed down to us two-hundred fifty times in the flood legends from all the world, is an archetype of the catastrophe of humanity and raises a series of theological questions, at least in the high cultures.

Can the God who created humanity be the same God as the one who destroys humanity? Is this a conflict in the divine? As the Babylonian Gilgamesh epic related in this conflict, the different gods were not agreed as to what should happen to the earth. In the council of the gods, the decree was issued to destroy humanity. "The heart of the great gods was inflamed with causing a great flood" (Gilgamesh II). However, the god Ea resisted and opposed the aggressive god Enlil insisting that other punishments like wild beasts, famines, and pestilence were more appropriate! After the flood the gods were horrified about what they had done. They separated themselves from Enlil, and the goddess Ishtar repented: "Oh, if only I had never decreed the great flood!" She swore: "In all eternity I will never forget this day."

Thus the contradiction in the Babylonian myth is ascribed to different gods, whereas in the Bible it is a contradiction in God. The creator and preserver is at the same time the judge and destroyer. How can this be? Does God change? Does God make plans that are abandoned? Is God not the eternal One, unchangeable, faithful, and unalterable? The Bible corrects this notion that we have of God. It corrects our enlightened deism, which allows us to speak of God more as an eternal law than as a personal being.

God cannot be severed from his partnership with us. God is not independent from us. God is capable of repentance, this especially human quality. According to Jewish tradition, repentance and conversion are central in the life of a person. There is nothing greater than repentance, says the Talmud. The rabbis declared that God invented repentance even before the world was formed. "Seven things were created before the universe came into existence: the law, repentance, paradise, the underworld, the throne of glory, the sanctuary, and the name of the Messiah." The world was created as a shrine for human beings and therefore had to be outfitted for their reception. In the law was the way to true life that humans should follow. There also had to be the possibility of life, the possibility of conversion, in case people deviated from the path of the law, and this was given through the possibility of repentance. Even God can do what is most crucial in Jewish tradition: to repent. People are capable of repentance; at any moment we can repent, that is, become human. Since God turns around and repents of the project, we should believe that every person, as violent as he or she may be, is capable of repentance.

Against Divine Imperialism

The God of the Bible is a God who repents and longs for our repentance. How does God relate to nature? Some think "creating" is the same as "making." What I make, I can also take away. If the earth is a great factory, then production can be shut down and creation ruined and undone. Can those be right who think it is God's will if the atom bomb falls, so that nothing can be done to avert this divine decree?

There is a masculine theology that imagines God as commander in chief, as omnipotence, and as emperor. I call this theology divine imperialism, since it functions in the sphere of ideology as imperialism acts in the economic and political sphere, namely, to subjugate people. The basic motif of divine imperialism for the relationship of God to people is dominion or superiority in power. This theology is fateful in a deep sense. God is only another word for saying: "It happens as it must happen." Our life is subject to the higher power.

What "God" does is done well. Believing in God in the sense of this imperialist theology means submitting to what is, just as one submits to bad weather, tax liability, and technological pressures. All things have their purpose, this piety proclaims, and cannot be otherwise. Thus fatalism is the reverse side of divine imperialism. God is the owner of the world and acts like owners who can do or not do with their property whatever they see fit. For many people possession and rule are the only categories of living relationships. We are only certain of "having" what we possess or rule. However, the Bible corrects this stony faith. God is not our owner. If God is our ruler, it is in a sense completely different from a fateful superior force. God does not "have" us in hand but enters with us into a covenant whose foundation is not the order of having but of being together and sharing life.

In our narrative of God's second creation under realistic conditions, God declares that the earth is not a divine possession, and God voluntarily surrenders the power to subject it to a flood or a nuclear winter. The earth lives its rhythm of seed and harvest, frost and heat, summer and winter, day and night. God will not be a Lord who interrupts this. I understand God's vow as listening to the earth. God does something that we've done sometimes as children: Laying an ear on the earth, God listens to its noises, its voices, its animals, and its movement. God is not only husband and possessor, commander and ruler. God confirms the creation: The earth shall retain its rhythms and its time. The earth shall yield seeds and harvests and shall not be buried under asphalt, poisoned, and steeped in waste. Frost and heat shall touch our bodies, so that our time is not spent in a continuously heated office. The earth shall remain the earth, despite those who sell and lease, plunder and destroy it.

Feminist theology sets out from the reciprocity and mutuality of all living relations and therefore criticizes the divine imperialism of the dominant theology. I quote from an essay that appeared in 1982 (V. Fritz, " 'So lange die Erde steht'—Vom Sinn der jahwistischen Fluterzählung in Gen. 6–8," *Zeitschrift für die alttestamentliche Wissenschaft* 94 [1982]: 609–10):

> Against the elemental inclination of humankind to evil, Yah-
> weh sets the promise in Gen. 8:22. Since the flood did not
> change the people in their mental constitution, Yahweh had
> to interrupt the deed-state connection. The curse of the earth
> ends, and the future existence of the whole earth is safe-
> guarded. A repetition of the flood is excluded, since Yahweh
> renounces this kind of punishment. The destruction of cre-
> ation is no longer anticipated. The responsibility of persons
> for their actions is not annulled, but individual fate takes the
> place of collective punishment. . . . As malice is punished,
> Yahweh can place this connection between guilt and punish-
> ment in a new setting. In any case, Yahweh remains beyond
> manipulation.

Like all emperors. The correspondence between divine imperialism and individualism is obvious. Fritz sums up his interpretation in the melancholy wisdom: "Thus the meaning of
the flood narrative can be understood from its end: although the people have not changed, they can no longer en-
danger the continuance of the world through their conduct"
(p. 614). Ergo: our industries may cheerfully continue to poison. God is the great solitary actor. Only for the individual is
there responsibility.

The dimension of an ideological obsessiveness of theological study can be discerned in V. Fritz's research. At the beginning of the 1970s the idea arose of making overpopulation
the motif of the great flood. The excessive multiplication of
people was described as the problematic background for the
Babylonian versions of the flood legend! This "interpretation"
reflects the fears and hopes of the technocratic power elite.

Deliverance

We know today how easy it is to curse the earth for the sake
of greedy profit, to turn it into raw material managed as
an imperialist rules subjugated lands. In this story of Noah,
the dove, and the olive branch, God proclaims a different

relationship with the earth. God is with the earth and sides with the abused earth, which is no longer to be cursed for the sake of people.

The famous verses 21 and 22 express in a theologically declamatory way what is related in our story. The dove flies.

Today we are called to keep God's covenant with the earth against the flood that threatens to destroy all things more dreadfully than the first time.

When we plead for the creation, we are in harmony with the oldest traditions of humanity, which all refuse to treat the earth as an object or as exploitable material. The earth is the Lord's, as the psalm says. In creation God entered the earth; thus we can say: The earth is holy. We do not possess it and are not its lords. In our story overcoming the owner mentality is revealed in God. The conflict between the different gods who have different relationships with the earth does not continue. Rather, it is God who repents of God's own plan. First of all, God intended to "strike" and "curse." Now there is a beginning of new life in God. God turns around.

Perhaps we have worshiped too long a cursing god under the name of technical progress, in which the earth was not holy but a kind of colony one plunders. We prescribed for ourselves whatever was greater, faster, and more. The God of the Yahwist (one of the biblical authors) was still in a position to change orientation and curse the earth no more. Will the god of Western progress change its views on subjugation of all life? Will the dove return with the olive branch in its beak? The images of peace help us to hope.

CHAPTER EIGHT

The Christmas Gospel: Luke 2:1–20

> When the angels had left them and gone into heaven, the shepherds said to one another, "Let us go now to Bethlehem and see this thing that has taken place, which the Lord has made known to us." So they went with haste and found Mary and Joseph, and the child lying in the manger. When they saw this, they made known what had been told them about this child; and all who heard it were amazed at what the shepherds told them. But Mary treasured all these words and pondered them in her heart. The shepherds returned, glorifying God for all they had heard and seen, as it had been told them.
>
> (Luke 2:15–20)

The Christmas narrative for me is a classical example for the productivity of sociohistorical biblical interpretation. Therefore I want to represent my story here with this story. For many years I was so disgusted by the commercialization that this fragment of religious tradition has endured, so sickened by the terror of consumption, the pressures of buying, giving, and eating, that I did not want even to think of Luke 2. The violent context in which we live had blocked the light of the text, which seemed to me hopelessly instrumentalized for lies. Neither the historical critical method nor an aesthetics shaped by the middle class of the nineteenth century helped me. The baby in the manger was embarrassing, like rich almond candy.

The escape of the yuppies—to run away and have a few beautiful days without fuss—was not available to me for family reasons. Instead we attempted to work in the context, to locate the stable in a homeless shelter in Cologne-Mülheim and to find the shepherds again among marginalized youths and vagabonds. They told the story in their way and thereby contributed to our liberation. The text itself remained a piece from the museum. That changed at the end of the seventies, when I learned something historically that had not occurred to me in study and exegesis.

I understood rather late what the tyranny of the *Imperium romanum* really meant for the people in the subjugated provinces. Up to this moment I held unsuspectingly to my humanist illusions about the *pax romana*. I regarded it as a kind of constitutional state with a cosmopolitan trading system and grandiose architecture. I had learned to read history only with the eyes of the victor. That the *pax Christi* was intended precisely for those who could expect nothing from the *pax romana* gave me a new key to the Christmas narrative and to the whole New Testament. How and under what conditions had people lived then in Galilee? Why had I never noticed the number of sick who appear in the Gospels? Who or what made them sick? Political oppression, legal degradation, economic plunder, and religious neutrality in the scope of the *religio licita* ("permitted religion") were realities that the writer Luke kept in view in his story, which is so sublime and yet so focused on the center of all conceivable power. At last I saw the *imperium* from the perspective of those dominated by it. I recognized torturers and informers behind the coercive measure, "All went . . . to be registered" (v. 3). Finally I comprehended the peace of the angels "on earth" and not only in the souls of individual people. I understood for the first time the propaganda terms of the Roman writers who spoke of *pax* and *jus* when they really meant grain prices and militarization of the earth known at that time. (All this can be confirmed by research today.)

Of course, my rereading was politically colored. I too was surrounded by propaganda (freedom and democracy). While I heard the boot of the empire crush everything in its way in the narrative from Bethlehem to Golgotha, I saw the carpet bombings in the poor districts of San Salvador right behind the glittering displays on Fifth Avenue in New York. The sociohistorical interpretation of biblical texts does not arise out of the abstraction of researchers who believe themselves neutral. It arises among people capable of suffering and compassion, who search for the causes of misery. In Paul these causes are called the reign of sin. Without understanding this *imperium* in its economic and ecological power of death, we also cannot see the light of Christmas shine. Living in the pretended social market economy, we do not even seem to need this light!

Whoever wants to proclaim something about this light has to free the stifled longing of people. Sociohistorical interpretation that takes seriously concrete everyday human cares and does not make the dying of children from hunger and neglect into a negligible quantity is helpful in this regard. By showing the organized violence—three billion German marks for the most massive deployment of military power since the Second World War—it deepens our yearning for true peace, which can have no other foundation than economic and ecological justice. This fundamental work of naming the alternative to the *pax romana* and to the model of present-day Germany is the task of the churches at Christmas.

Our text (verses 15–20) refers to the praxis of transmission and proclamation. The frightened shepherds become God's messengers. They organize, make haste, find others, and speak with them. Do we not all want to become shepherds and catch sight of the angel? I think so. Without the perspective of the poor, we see nothing, not even an angel. When we approach the poor, our values and goals change. The child appears in many other children. Mary also seeks sanctuary among us. Because the angels sing, the shepherds rise, leave their fears behind, and set out for Bethlehem, wherever it is situated these days. The historic new beginning of 1990 [German reunification] does not represent the definitive farewell to the utopias, to spiritless life without angels, in which the poor shepherds are finally made invisible.

On the contrary, we can now take the side of the poor without false compassion or distraction; we can become shepherds and hear the angels sing.

> "Glory to God in the highest heaven,
> and on earth peace among those whom God favors!"

PART IV
Transformations

CHAPTER NINE

In Search of a
New Religious Language

Between Scientific and Everyday Language

The helplessness and weakness of current religious language is obvious. Religious discourse appears antiquated, unintelligible, or at best conventional and without communicative value. "Merciful?" a female student asked me in a literature seminar. "Is that a printing error? Does it mean genial? Or friendly?" I could name many other religious ideas, sin and grace, for example, which have a reduced meaning in certain everyday contexts and are unintelligible in their religious significance.

Religious language shares this fate of progressive pauperization with human language in general and technical language in particular. A language is taught and practiced that unites the highest precision with total desubjectivization, the language of science, which approaches mathematical abstraction in an ideal typical way. This language is normative and exercises dominion over the "pre"-scientific, nonprofessional language of everyday life, which for its part is impoverished and shallow. The regional dialects with their original riches and wit are replaced by the standardized language of the mass media. The language of feelings is exposed to a destructive process of trivialization by advertising. Scientific language does not nourish or enrich this everyday language and does nothing to oppose this process of trivialization; it remains aloof. Scientific language dominates by forcing people to use its language and no other. In this sense the living space for a human language becomes smaller and more private. The person caught between scientific and everyday language is not assisted by its formulations. What the language of the classicists achieved for a long time and what Brecht attempted in our century, namely, expanding an intermediate area where people can express themselves humanly and holistically, seems more and more difficult.

In this precarious situation, religious language also degenerates into advertising jargon on the one hand ("Give Jesus a try") and abstract theology on the other. Franz Kafka said: "A book must be like an ax in order to break the ice of the soul."

Even "theology" is largely frozen in our context. The word itself has experienced an enormous inflation, which is connected with the scientific expression and the professionalization of theology. The existential character of true theology often perishes in the scientific enterprise, and there is a danger that the handmaid, science, may make herself the ruler of theology.

Three Forms of Religious Language

The language lost to us is not the language of theology but an existential language whose forms include prayer and narrative. Religion is expressed on three different planes: mythic- narrative, religious-confessional, and argumentative- reflective. For example, the phenomenon of human suffering, guilt, privation, and the finiteness of life can be discussed in very different ways. We can narrate the myth of the garden of paradise and the expulsion of the first humans, Adam and Eve. This is a picturesque story that evokes thoughts and feelings without interpretation. Second, we can appropriate subjectively the fate of guilt and hostility and express this religiously in the concept of "sin." Paul Ricoeur emphasized this transition from mythical fate to religious sin. The third kind of speaking is theological-philosophical reflection that seeks to comprehend guilt in the dogma of original sin.

Telling a story, making a confession, and building an idea are very different forms of religious interpretation of the world, which we identify with the words *myth, religion,* and *theology.* To the secular mind these intrareligious distinctions are rather meaningless. The three ideas are often used in an indiscriminate and deprecatory way. Mass atheism may be right: It is only a question of different language games with the same theme.

In regard to these three forms of language, the religiocritical tradition of the Enlightenment takes a historicizing position that believes in progress. People believe that an irreversible development from myth to Logos occurs in the course of time and can be stated in concepts. The Logos as the stage of progressive consciousness supersedes myth by reducing it to an idea. But is it true that in the course of time myth, through religion, dies in the Logos? There are good reasons today to deny the thesis of progressive secularization. In spite of enlightened thought, religion has not made itself superfluous; it has not become insignificant for human decisions. We come nearer the truth of religious consciousness, it seems to me, when we regard it as sharing simultaneously in the three forms of religious expression. I would like to propose the following thesis: Contemporary, or postenlightened, theology has to share in all three planes of religious language.

Without the narrative element, which includes retelling myths and narrating particular experiences, theology dries up. At the same time it becomes masculinized into a life-threatening absolute sexism. By this I do not mean only that in this theology women have nothing to say and must be discriminated against in institutions and in writing. I think rather that the theological method of male appropriation of the world leaves out the narrative. It is violated from the beginning in the concept. The sexism of the theology dominant in the church and the university consists not only in the unconscious assumption that humankind is male but also in the complete eradication of the mythic-narrative.

Successful theology has always practiced narration and prayer; it shares in all three planes of religious discourse. It invites myth to return. Its linguistic form, narrative and prayer, is sought, not banished as impure. By the way, this is a criterion of liberation theology, whether black, feminist, or devoted to the poor.

Everywhere there is narration and lament, which is one form of prayer; witnesses and lecturers appear at the great conferences of the *oikumene*. When Domitila, the Bolivian miner's wife, told of the hunger strike of Bolivian housewives, what she did was to relate and to conjure up, to plead and to accuse, to analyze and to reflect. What she said cannot be summarized; prayer and narrative would be barred in this form of communication and would die in its coldness. A new synthesis of myth, religion, and reflection is arising today wherever theology has a liberating character. Myth is not artificially protected from the grip of the Logos, as religious orthodoxy attempted. Rather, it is criticized where it legitimates the rule of people over people in the sense of sexism or racism. Myth is not destroyed when we see its functions in a particular situation.

Nor is myth superfluous in the Logos. Rather, it is asserted, celebrated, and repeated. The strongest testimonies of liberation theology are prayers, liturgies, and worship services that dramatize Christian myth, most importantly the exodus and the resurrection. That can happen only among groups that are intent on changing the world and do not distance themselves in a resigned, academic way from such undertakings. They need God because the dominant interpretation of "this world" represents a death sentence for the poor. The poor have to become poorer, so that the rich can become richer. It is an illusion to assume that we live in a scientifically surveyable and controllable world that can renounce interpretations such as that of God as justice. Only the rich can comfortably renounce God. The return of myth occurs among those who need its hope.

There is a theology without poetry that through various mechanisms seals itself against the renewal of language. Sentences that are "theopoetic" (envisioning God poetically) are dismissed as "merely literary" and distinguished from the supposedly theological. Dogmatic thought—that is, traditional systems of dogmatics and the uncodified dogmatism that is no longer capable of its own dogmatic formation but is constantly setting up intellectual prohibitions and taboos—serves as a system of protection. The legalism of theology and its institutions is another attempt to protect faith from poetry. In nearly all the disputes between Christians and church administrators, legalist language is used "from above" against original theopoetic declarations; the language of God is not renewed. The most important wall that unpoetic theology has erected against renewal and change is the enslavement of theology to science, in which attempts to crack the ice of the soul are themselves subject to the freezing process. Obviously, critical reason has a place in theology and performs a necessary function against superstition and biblicism. But those who command only the language of science remain ignorant in essential relationships. Today enlightened language is no longer sufficient for the enlightened consciousness, since it cannot articulate specific experiences, for example, absurdity or meaning, alienation or solidarity with all that lives. Its greatest weakness is that it isolates us from myth, religion, and poetry and suffocates our mythic, religious, poetic nature.

Merely rational language is not enough. It is too small for our needs. It explains but does not satisfy. It "enlightens"—even if seldom—but does not warm. It defines, sets limits, criticizes, makes possible distinctions, but the most important work, namely, communication, is not attempted in this language. At best, enlightenment spares the area where we can share life together. At best, the language of enlightenment protects the place and time in which we touch and share together the sanctity of life. It resists the destruction of life. It forbids our making an image, likeness, or ideology of God. This is absolutely necessary. It helps us see that neither "practical constraints" nor the "total market" nor "security" is the ultimate, unquestionable reality to which we can subordinate everything else. The language of enlightenment does not say what it means to love God above all things.

It seems that the question of truth can no longer be raised within the historical world and that it is completely impossible to answer it with the help of science. A new search for myth and religious assurance—in the widest sense of the word—is beginning.

This discussion is new, because the science that should supersede myth no longer bears the burden of explaining and organizing the world, at least not for the most sensitive among us. With the limits of growth, the limits of science and its world responsibility have also become clear to us. In the crisis of science, which, for example, the theologian Rudolf Bultmann, as well as his contemporary Bert Brecht, did not perceive, the question of myth is raised again. Is myth, the story of the invasion of divine energies into human reality, necessary for expressing the future or even a hope for the world?

Religious language can teach us to identify our feelings, to know ourselves and make ourselves known. There is a shallowness free of religion that is also directed against poetry. Language itself, which is full of remembrance, opposes that shallowness. In language we do not only encounter ourselves and express our actuality. We always live in a house of language built by generations before us. Therefore the remembrance of another life and the hope for less destructive methodologies can hardly be eradicated.

Why Is a New Language Necessary?

The connection between poetic and religious language is clear to me in its opposite: the new speechlessness of a family that no longer eats together. Each takes from the refrigerator what he or she needs, the young watch television up to six hours a day, and there is no conversation anymore.

Our own language is destroyed and corrupted. When a word like *love* is applied to the car, or a word like *purity* to a special detergent; these words have no meaning anymore but are destroyed. All the words that express feelings are damaged for us, including religious language. "Jesus Christ is our Redeemer"—this is ritualized, destroyed language that is dead. There are many people who can no longer say what they want to say or what they expect from life. I believe that writing involves a certain despair of the old language, a certain loathing. Shame is a revolutionary sensation, as Marx said. We must be ashamed how language is chattered and destroyed, how people are destroyed or cannot find themselves at all in what is said. In this shame I am trying to find the language we need. A first presupposition of writing and speaking today is that we resist envelopment by the media and withdraw from their laws. These laws dominate our thinking and destroy our ability to hope or—to speak biblically—to see the world with the eyes of Jesus.

The media under which we live and perceive reality represent a selection, which is always ahead of us and always more powerful than what we "see" ourselves. They incapacitate us and train us to regard our own life as trivial, uninteresting, and unimportant. Living under these coercions, we find that myth, a story interpreting the world in relation to God, is a help. Myth reminds us that our story can also be told differently, that our relationship to the world is different from what the masters of our consciousness believe. A *star* is not just a celestial body when the people who walked in darkness see "a great light."

The mythic-narrative language of the Bible resists the pressures of the media and criticizes one of their fundamental presuppositions: absolute faith in power and success. One of the communicated messages that we receive from the media is that only success counts. What is not successful now—however true it may be—does not get into the program. The sanctity of life, for which I have tried to plead here, is consistently and mercilessly destroyed in the rituals of consumerism.

The ancient myth is the narration of the fact that life is holy. This holiness has to be dramatized again and again, so that we do not forget it or consider it superfluous. In mythical language we give thanks for the sun, bless the bread, wish one another a safe journey home, and remember that life is a gift, not a possession. The widow with the two pennies is such a dramatization.

Communicating God

What do prayer and poetry have in common? They connect us with our hopes. They take us out of hopeless misery. They remind us of our purpose.

The dangers of all the symbols of the rationalist technical world are evident today at the end of this epoch. Is a turnaround possible in which the poetry banished as merely feminine returns home? Will the "mother tongue of the human family" (G. F. Hamann, 1762) creep into the technological father jargon and heal us? Is language only an instrument of world domination, ultimately an expression of the "will to power," which one could study perfectly in Ronald Reagan's speeches? Theology and poetry, the language of desire and hope, lament and prayer are similarly threatened.

Theology and poetry have more in common today than ever. Both are outcasts; both are regarded as insignificant. In the schools and training institutes, one can refuse to learn these languages. Passive appropriation is still endured; everything that goes beyond the mere reception of a cultural inheritance is questioned. Who then can write poetry and teach prayer? Who would do what poetry and prayer repeatedly attempt, to communicate God, to share God, and to spread the goodness that communicates itself?

In a language world that is governed by consumerism, we can only express ourselves in the categories of possession. Our relation to the world is defined by the most important idols that our culture worships: money and power. This means literally that many people fall into a strange helplessness toward everything that cannot be acquired, managed, purchased, conquered, possessed, controlled, and commercialized. The dominating language of possession, including the divided language of being and a helpless stammering that we know in bereavement, is still the best that those made speechless accomplish.

"The human lives poetically," said Hölderlin, nourished by poetry and prayer. Whenever we escape the language of domination and attempt another language—that is, learn to hear, understand, and speak another language—the linguistic creation, the new development of language, is a source of power and an encouragement that extends far beyond analytical and critical knowledge. I remember how I first heard the maxim, "Gentle water breaks the stone." This saying reminds us of what gentle water has already done, of Brecht's poem about the genesis of the book *Tao Te Ching*, a word of vision, a sentence that speaks of what the Bible calls the "strength of the weak," a theopoetic sentence, a sentence that does not make a statement about time or answer the obvious question: "When, finally?" The sentence between remembrance and vision reminds me that I will probably die before the stone is broken and the war in which we now live is ended, this war against the poorest of this world, against the creation, and against ourselves. To sing of peace in the midst of war, I believe, was the secret of the people in the New Testament, who trembled under a comparable misanthropic empire and sang their different songs. Thus they "lived poetically" and shared with each other a different language.

CHAPTER TEN

Freedom as Thirst for Liberation

> Now the Lord is the Spirit, and where the Spirit of the
> Lord is, there is freedom.
>
> (2 Cor. 3:17)

Another translation reads:

> The Spirit is the effect of the Messiah on us. He alone
> determines our life. Where his Spirit is, freedom rules.

These are great words: *Spirit, pneuma, life, freedom, eleutheria.* "Ubi autem spiritus domini, ibi libertas"—there is freedom. The question to all the great nouns is the question the Polish philosopher Stanislaus Lec raised: "Liberty, equality, fraternity—very beautiful! But how do we get to the verbs?" How can we move from nouns to deeds, to action? What are the correct verbs to go with *Spirit* and *freedom?* What are the verbs we actually need?

I want to try to see how Paul went from *Spirit* and *freedom* to the verbs. I will take the roundabout way that the Christian tradition suggests to me, because I am mindful of the hidden way of the Spirit among us.

For most of ancient Christendom, the experience of being grasped by God's Spirit was fundamental. All these ancient Christians experienced the *pneuma* as God's power in their lives, transforming them, healing them, comforting them, and encouraging them. The power of ecstasy inheres in the power of miracles, for example, in the healing of the lame, which surpasses our usual division into the spiritual, inner reality, forgiveness of sins, and outward, physical, material reality. Jesus always healed both, the spirit and the body.

The power of the Spirit in this first community was experienced as speaking in tongues and healing of the sick, which not only Jesus but also his disciples did as demon exorcisms. These were signs of the penetration of the Spirit. People who confessed Christ lived differently from the way they had lived before they knew him. They lived in a new form of cooperative life. They related differently to one another. Pagan writers described this and said again and again: "Behold, how they love one another!" It was striking in the world of that time when people dealt differently with two realities: one reality was money and property, and the other reality was the authority that "wielded the sword."

These two realities were lived differently by the first Christians. They had all things in common and refused military service and cooperation with the war machinery. These were the two decisive points that changed when Christ came into their lives. We must imagine the life of these people with all their difficulties. It was life under a great power but not in the heart of this great power, not in Rome, not amid free Roman citizens who had all the luxuries that this great power provided for the elite, but at the edge of this great power, on the periphery, in the many subjugated, militarily occupied, and economically exploited lands ruled by Rome.

The system under which the people in the New Testament lived was the "peace of Rome," the *pax romana*, as named by its own extollers. It was a political and economic system that served to make the people in the center of this system—namely, in Rome—richer and the subjugated people outside this system poorer. Almost all the wars at that time, such as the wars against Carthage, were economic wars. Grain prices were crucial, and Rome sought to assert its power and fix the prices. That was the peace of Rome. It was guaranteed by an excellently organized military system and facilitated by state-of-the-art road construction. "If you want peace, prepare for war," said one of the philosophers of this military system—a rule that still seems valid for many today.

Nevertheless, extreme misery prevailed within this *pax romana*. When you consider the New Testament as a whole, it is truly astonishing how many sick persons abound, how there are the gravely and incurably ill, the paralyzed, and the psychically ill, who are connected with demons, on nearly every page of this book. Sickness, misery, despair, and hopelessness seethed everywhere on the edges of this empire, where the poor lived.

Into this world Christ comes and proclaims a different peace: the *pax Christi*, the peace of Christ; he proclaims liberation for the poor and a different Spirit. It is no longer the spirit of mourning and weariness, of divine resignation—"as it was, so it will always be"—but a new and different Spirit: "Now the Lord is the Spirit, and where the Spirit of the Lord is, there is freedom," Paul declares.

The oldest Christians prayed for this Spirit. It defined their lives; it determined their association with one another and with the realities of existence. They prayed for Christ's Spirit to strengthen them. I imagine that like us they often lived dull, dispirited, indifferent, mundane lives and then prayed for the Spirit: "Come Holy Spirit, abide with us!"

People who say seriously that they experience dullness or mindlessness—an experience that comes to every reflective person—have a longing to be touched and moved by the Spirit. This experience is present in the yearning to be seized by the Spirit. One of the most beautiful words of the German language, which does not appear in this form in other languages, is the word *Begeisterung* (inspiration, enthusiasm), which is used again and again by Goethe's friend Johann Gottfried Herder. Without inspiration, says Herder, nothing important is created—without the experience of being borne by the Spirit, being overcome by the Spirit, and living in God's Spirit. Nothing good or beautiful has come into the world without this kind of *in*-spiration.

I would like to reflect this in another culture that has taught me a great deal, the culture of the blacks in North America, who in their songs and spirituals so often sing of the Spirit and are also able in the negative sense to articulate lack of Spirit. There is an expression when one is not at all well, when nothing is really going right and one feels miserable and wretched: "Ain't got no spirit!" The Spirit is not there; something is missing that gives a spark to life and makes it worth living. This is an expression of emptiness and mere functioning with which we can operate a very long time: eating, drinking, acting, settling affairs, doing our work and everything possible, and still, "Ain't got no spirit!"

There is a spiritual that begins with the words, "Every time I feel the Spirit moving in my heart. . . ." When I hear this song, I ask myself when was the last time I felt the Spirit? And I would like to ask you: When was the last time you felt the Spirit move—on what occasion, where, why, when? The song "Every time I feel the Spirit moving in my heart" awakens my spiritual hunger, the hunger without which we can, of course, vegetate but not live.

"Where the Spirit of the Lord is, there is freedom." Paul had to wage a conflict on two fronts over the inspiration of the Spirit in the early community. On the one hand, he resisted the church's domestication of the Spirit, and on the other, he carried on a kind of battle with fanatics and enthusiasts. Thus there is a struggle against the underspirited and a struggle against the overspirited. Those who are without spirit and the ecclesiastical tamers of the Spirit are interested in order above all. Their focus is on the institution and order. They prefer to interpret our text as follows: "Where the Spirit of the Lord is, there is order!" The worship service runs by rote, women are silent in church, and the verbs that belong to this kind of spirit are *preserve, conserve, guard*, and *defend*. The revolutionary spirit of the gospel—its fundamental criticism of property and violence, its criticism of military force and supreme power—is silenced. Instead, the ordering—not spiritless but still—spirit-avoiding institution is desired. An ecclesiastical domestication of spirits began that later led people to believe long after Paul that life under the customs and rule of Rome, that is, under the spirit of the *pax romana*, could be reconciled and integrated with the Spirit of Christ. It was as though one could be faithful to Christ's Spirit and use his Spirit for the inner soul, for our moments of despair and our fears, but simultaneously serve another spirit, the spirit of the *pax romana* based on property and power, for the outward life and our progress in this life. I do not believe it is possible to domesticate, dam up, and trivialize the Spirit in this sense and subject it to an order. "Where the Spirit of the Lord is, there is freedom."

On the other hand, Paul criticizes the overzealous enthusiasts, who are so far removed from reality that they believe they can leap over it in a kind of drunkenness of the Spirit. Paul reminds his Corinthian community that all things depend on the Spirit of Christ. How is this Spirit distinguished from other spirits? Since a great many run about in Christ's name and write Christ on their banners, we can hardly know what spirit really underlies their activity, even if the words are the same—no more than we can know whether it is really God whose name is written on every dollar: "IN GOD WE TRUST," whether it is the Father of Jesus Christ or perhaps another god. This is also true with the Spirit of Christ.

Paul reminds the Corinthians that all things depend on Christ's Spirit. He distinguishes this Spirit by his decisive criterion, the cross, and the affirmation and acceptance of suffering, with the understanding that our following this Christ brings difficulties, plunges us into conflict, makes us different, offers no guarantee of success, but exacts a wholly different life from us. The overzealous like to ignore the bloody reality that the *Imperium romanum* excludes and oppresses, exiles and discriminates, and in the worst cases punishes, tortures, and ultimately kills all who seek to fulfill God's will and to live God's justice.

This was the reality of the world at that time. Those who held to Christ had to prepare themselves for the likelihood that Christ would be seized and killed by the empire. We cannot really understand the New Testament if we do not see how the people who spoke of God's Spirit and acted for justice and peace had to expect death as a reward. The Christ who lived in these people was at the same time the Christ who hung on the cross. Paul reminded his community in Corinth of this.

I imagine these unsuffering enthusiasts were a little like today's adherents of the New Age. "Where the Spirit of God is," they say, "there is harmony, there we feel wholeness, there is light in us, and hunger and everything caused by hunger do not appear at all." Then we bypass Christ's way to God and avoid this dreadful, bloody, brutal reality that we describe with the symbol of the cross, the ancient symbol of torture.

Where the Spirit of God is, many think today, I feel extremely good. There I have everything together; there I can realize myself. Is that the Spirit of God? No, says Paul. The Spirit of Christ is more than self-realization. Where this Spirit is, there is a different freedom. This freedom is greater than the freedom of the new consciousness, which deludes with false hopes that the arms industry, the bomb industry, and the impoverishment of the poor will collapse tomorrow wholly of themselves if we only have the right spirit in us. Entirely without a struggle, merely through inner consciousness, the abhorrent realities of this world will fall away. This is a dream, the dream of this gentle conspiracy. I believe that Paul with good reason warned against reducing the Spirit of Christ, so to speak, and making it a spirit of harmony, joy, and enthusiasm alone, without observing the reality of the cross. Paul declared that where the Spirit of Christ rules in us, there is not pure sunshine but freedom.

What is freedom? I have meditated over this word's meaning for me in the last ten years and how it has changed. Great words shrink mostly when they are left behind and do not grow with us. Then they lose their true substance and become husks, comic-strip balloons for any and all politicians, and they do not mean anything anymore. For me the word *freedom* has become an increasingly important word. I think every generation has the right to redefine this word. And if it has the right, it also has the duty. After having worked long in the European and transatlantic peace movement, I believe that freedom, a deeper inner idea of freedom, will not be attained until we are free of bombs, free of poison gas, free of the arms industry, and free of this whole cancer that overruns our entire life, defines our cities, rules our research, and terrorizes our landscapes with its low-flying aircraft that cause schoolchildren to scream and cry at night because they are so disturbed.

Freedom, true freedom, has become for me an intense yearning for a freedom from the most dreadful scourge of humanity, war. This is not a utopian dream. For centuries people said again and again: "Slavery is a necessary economic reality and has to continue. Without slavery the cotton industry in the American South will collapse. Without slavery—we can shape it somewhat more humanely, of course, since we are all for it—nothing works."

One day people will speak about war and preparation for war as we speak today about slavery. Perhaps the day will come when people understand that we can live without nuclear slavery, without conventional slavery, without chemical slavery, and without all the forms of this slavery that claim our minds and use us for their madness—fifty-one percent of all scientists and engineers work for death within the first world. I believe that we define freedom correctly when our ideas grow with us and are not left behind, that is, when our own intellectual growth, our judgment, capacity for truth, and search for truth develop so that we have different ideas with more reality. Thus I would like most to pray: "Free me, O God, from the dreadful historical role of the middle class in rich countries. Let my thirst for liberation grow."

It has become clearer and clearer to me that freedom is always liberation. As soon as it congeals into a word composed with the suffix -dom and no longer has the character of "more freedom," greater freedom, which sees the prisons more exactly, even our own prisons—as soon as this character is lost, freedom stiffens into a kind of ideology. But where the Spirit of God is, there is liberation: *liberación*, not only *libertas* but the process of liberation. The more the Spirit of God we have, the more visible become the prisons in which we live, on which we build, and in which we let others go to ruin. I cannot reduce my desire for liberation, for example, to the instrument of free elections, as though all that is promised us as freedom is to vote freely once every four years in a free land. That is a shameless reduction of reality, a reduction of what freedom can really mean. Freedom includes becoming free in our research and in our expenditures. For example, a country without prisons or with fewer prisons would be free. The great American socialist Eugene Debs said at the beginning of this century: "As long as there is a working class, I am a member. As long as there is only one soul in prison, I am not free." I find something of Christ's Spirit in these sentences, the Spirit that does not privately claim freedom for oneself but understands that we all belong together. As long as someone is still in prison, I am not free.

Where the Spirit is, there grows liberation. There grow also the combative desire for liberation and the experience of greater concrete freedom, which are not yet visible in our violent conditions.

I would like to live differently from the way I now live. I would like not to cheat people in other countries when I buy bananas by defrauding them of their wages. I would like not to steal when I drink coffee. I do not want to belong to this band of murderers and thieves that our economy represents. I do not want hunger to continue forever. I do not want to live in a system that has proven itself unable to alter hunger in the last thirty years, a system that has not really worked on this problem anywhere in the world, but instead makes weapons, weapons, weapons. I am not free as long as I live in these conditions.

One understands the real social movements in our world, the movements for more justice, more peace, and the integrity of creation, only when one understands them as longings for freedom. Where the Spirit of Christ is, there is freedom. There is liberation for all people, not only for us. Where do we find this Spirit in our world—in our part of the calm, sated, so-called peaceful free world? I will not give an answer here to this question; you have to find the answer yourself. There is no other way. We live in a prison because we build prisons. We still live in destruction because we are involved in the exploitation of others and profit from it. As long as we treat our mother earth as we do, where we exterminate another species of life, another of our brothers and sisters, plants, or animals every day, we are not free and the Spirit of Christ is not with us. This is simply obvious. Paul says: "Where the Spirit of the Lord is, there is freedom." I understand this to mean that since people long in a deeper sense for freedom, they cannot be fed with these verbal husks of freedom. They want true freedom. They pray for freedom, and they act in hope and in prayer for a greater freedom—the freedom that God gives us. Amen.

Prayer Based on
the Ninetieth Psalm

Lord, you have been our dwelling place in all generations!
Before the mountains were brought forth and the oceans,
before our little blue planet,
on which life multiplies through love and union,
was born from you after a long pregnancy,
you were there waiting for us.
You allow cultures to perish
when they separate from you,
and call others into being.
What seemed to us a thousand years and unchanging,
the bloody violence,
is to you a short watch in the night.
Even tyrants break down exhausted,
economic conglomerates dissolve,
and the knowledge of infallible parties
becomes last year's snow.
Slavery was profitable and flourished,
but in the evening of your day it withered.
The fruits of armament climbed to the sky,
but your anger consumed them,
and your wrath will destroy the stolen prosperity.
You make known our plundering of the poor;
you bring to light our veiled crimes.
Our days pass away quickly in fear of the truth;
we spend our years as if on a drug trip
that turns into horror.

Our life here is seventy years;
in other lands many will not live even four years.
Here we push eighty and more,
but joy has become stale;
technology drags us along.
Who has faith in you, poor God,
without nuclear bombs and without banks,
and who is afraid when your fish die?
Remind us that we are small,
dwelling here briefly on borrowed earth.
Teach us that we must die
and have no time for all the hatred
that makes our low-flying planes howl.
Teach us to number the days
in which we think of you
and call upon you.

Turn your countenance to us, O God;
come to those who watch for you.
Satisfy us in the morning with your light,
so that we make music, and no day is without joy.
Make us glad again after all the years of emptiness
in the land of looters,
where blood cleaves to our bank-palaces.
Bring us bread and roses, O God;
your splendor is in the hair of children.
Let your light be upon us, making it easy for us
to come and go.
Help us preserve your world
and establish the work of our hands,
the good work of liberation.